ATTICUS WEAVER

and His Triumphant Leap
from Outcast to Hero
and Back Again

by Alexandra Powe Allred

SUMMIT BOOKS

Perfection Learning®

Cover Illustration: Dan Hatala

Dedication:
To Kerri, Katie, and Tommy:
Always remember who you are.

For information, contact
Perfection Learning® Corporation
1000 North Second Avenue, P.O. Box 500
Logan, Iowa 51546-0500.
Phone: 1-800-831-4190
Fax: 1-800-543-2745
perfectionlearning.com

Paperback ISBN 0-7891-5935-x
Cover Craft® ISBN 0-7569-1202-4
2 3 4 5 6 PP 06 05

About the Author

Alexandra Powe Allred has a B.A. from Texas A & M University, where she majored in history and minored in Russian. As the daughter of a U.S. diplomat, Allred spent many years overseas, in Russia, Tunisia, Iraq, and Germany.

In 1994, she was named Athlete of the Year by the U.S. Olympic Committee and won a gold medal at the U.S. Nationals in women's bobsledding.

She is the author of several sports books including *The Quiet Storm* and *Atta Girl!* In addition, she has written *The Code, Entering the Mother Zone, Passion Rules! Inspiring Women in Business*, and a dog obedience book.

Currently, Allred maintains her passion for sports as a professional football player for the WPFL's Austin Rage. She is raising three young children with her husband, Robb.

Table of Contents

WHERE TO BEGIN?

WHEN asked to explain himself, he couldn't think of where to begin. It was still all so jumbled in his mind. His mother had told him, "Just start from the beginning," as though it were that simple. But what was the beginning? He really couldn't remember when it had all begun. Was it the new computer? Was it when they chased him? Or was it when everyone found out that Kevin Thurston would never again play ball for the Cougars?

No, it was before that. To understand why a kid like Atticus Weaver would bother to help a kid like Kevin Thurston, you would have to know about the wheelchair. You would have to know why it was so hard going through Mark Twain Elementary and Walnut Middle School with a name like *Atticus*.

The beginning, Atticus decided, started when he was just a baby. *Why* he couldn't walk didn't really matter. The fact was he couldn't walk. He'd been asked if he had multiple sclerosis, but that was more of a grown-up disease that attacked people in their early twenties. His was a condition he had been born with, and it didn't matter how many times he explained this. Kids always acted as though it were a secret that no one was supposed to know about, including Atticus. They would look at everything except his wheelchair, pretending it didn't exist. In Atticus's world, this was far worse than asking him what was wrong. So Atticus just stopped talking about it. There was no sense crying or complaining about it. It wasn't as if he knew any other way. He had never run before and didn't know what it felt like, so it was hard to know what he was missing. True, he would never be a football player. He would never be able to run and play like other children. But, he reasoned, he had other strengths. That was why his mother had decided that he should have a name so grand and noble that he would be respected for other things.

But—*Atticus?*

Atticus could think of plenty of other noble names besides *Atticus*. So, he thought, it was very likely that getting a name like Atticus was the very beginning of things to come.

Atticus Finch was the name of a character in the book *To Kill a Mockingbird.* He was a strong and honorable man. He was a lawyer who defended a black man unjustly accused of a crime he did not commit. Atticus Finch was well-read, well-spoken, strong, handsome, and kind. "All the things you are," Mrs. Weaver told her son when he asked why she had named him *Atticus*.

Yes, Atticus thought, but Atticus Finch lived in the days when people were named things like *Atticus* and *Harry* and *Cornelius*. Times were different now. Now those were exactly the kinds of names that could get you beat up after school. In fact, Atticus was sure that the only thing that saved him from getting beat up was the very fact that he was in a wheelchair. Otherwise, he was sure, he would be dead meat.

In the case of Kevin Thurston, however, even the wheelchair was not enough. Kevin had teased and tormented Atticus from almost the first day he heard Atticus's name in roll call. From his first day of attending Mark Twain Elementary in the fifth grade all the way through to the ninth grade at Walnut Middle School, Kevin Thurston and his thug friends had made things as difficult as they could for Atticus.

Atticus liked to study, and schoolwork was one thing he could do better than anyone. He excelled in math, science, and history. He loved computers, biology, and chess. He liked anything that involved using his greatest muscle—his brain. That, he knew, was something that his condition could never touch.

But the fact that school was the place where everyone made fun of his name and where he had to face Kevin and his friends every day made Atticus hate going. He would plead with his mother to let him stay home.

"You don't understand what it's like in school," he would tell her.

"Oh, it wasn't so long ago that I was in school myself," she would answer back, so sure she understood how it felt to be Atticus Weaver.

But if she really knew, if she really remembered how mean kids could be, she would have never named her kid Atticus Weaver. Atticus! He never understood why parents named their kids dumb names, just knowing they were going to be teased all the time. Sure, there were a lot of professional football players with dumb names, but when you're over six feet tall and weigh as much as a refrigerator, people don't make fun of you.

"Ah, yes," said Mrs. Weaver, waving a finger in the air. "But they were kids once too. Don't forget that!"

What she didn't acknowledge, however, was

that the dumb names and the teasing were precisely *why* they grew up to be mean football players. At least, this was what Atticus thought.

Adults always asked Atticus if it was a family name or something. They would say things like "*Atticus?* How interesting!" But the kids just wrinkled up their noses and wondered how come he got such a stupid name from his parents.

Mrs. Weaver kept trying to tell Atticus about the *To Kill a Mockingbird* thing. "But no one but us has ever heard of that book!" he would tell her.

"Just you wait. Every kid has to read that book in high school. It's a classic. Then they'll know what a great name you have."

Well, that's just great, Atticus would sigh. The whole name thing would be cleared up in a few short years. But when you are trying to make it through the day without getting chased down the hall for having a weird name or wearing glasses or whatever reason kids feel like picking on you, a few years could be a lifetime. And a lifetime with Kevin Thurston on your back was not something Atticus wanted to endure.

If parents really want to name their kids a great name that people will not understand the meaning of until they are almost adults, there needs to be some kind of rule in the hospital. "Okay, you can name your kid Cornelius or Atticus or Pumpernickel, but until he turns 15, you must call him *Joe*." There might be fewer football players in the world, but all in all, Atticus reasoned, there would be a whole lot more happy kids.

The only person who didn't seem to make Atticus feel different was his best friend, Trevor Smith. Trevor was also a bit of a mystery to Atticus. There wasn't anything, well, *wrong* with Trevor, but he wasn't very well liked. To Atticus, that just showed how stupid kids could be. Sometimes a kid was unpopular for no reason at all. Trevor was a good student, but he wasn't the brain of the school. That position was held by Atticus, and it was rightfully earned.

Trevor wasn't the tallest or the smallest. He wasn't the loudest or the quietest. He didn't have big feet or big ears. He didn't have a funny nose or a strange name. He wasn't a weakling, but he wasn't the strongest either. That position was held by Kevin and his buddies. Trevor was a good athlete and a good student. He came from a nice family. They weren't poor. They weren't rich. He was just a normal-looking, normal-acting kid—and Kevin Thurston had it in for Trevor big-time.

There *was* one thing that Trevor could do better than Kevin Thurston, better than anyone. Trevor Smith was the fastest runner anyone at Walnut Middle School had ever seen. He could outrun anyone. He could outrun Kevin and his gang, and that made Kevin furious. But that wasn't why he hated Trevor. Kevin had hated Trevor long before anyone knew how fast Trevor could run. In fact, that was exactly how everyone found out that Trevor *could* run.

Thinking about how he met Trevor Smith made Atticus pause—perhaps *that* was the beginning. It was the alliance between Trevor and Atticus that had helped Atticus clear Kevin's name. It was because of his friendship with Trevor that Atticus had gotten a computer. It was because of Trevor that Atticus came to terms with his own name and understood the power of it. It made sense that his friendship with Trevor could have been the beginning of everything. Without Trevor, there would have been nothing.

Atticus could remember it like it was yesterday—the expression on Kevin's face when Trevor Smith burst through the crowd and flew past him. Trevor was moving at what seemed like a hundred miles an hour. Kevin had never had a chance to react. In fact, no one had. It was, in some ways, Walnut Middle School's introduction to Trevor Smith. Before that, no one had even noticed he was around.

Kevin Thurston was the kind of kid who would pick on a new kid just for being new. Like a lion preying on a sick antelope, Kevin would strike. He knew the new kid had no friends to help. The new kid would just have to take whatever punishment Kevin dealt out until, at last, someone would feel sorry for him and come to the rescue, inviting him to sit at a certain lunch table or something. It was for that reason Trevor told Atticus that he would help him out when he saw Kevin taunting him.

"But not 'cause I feel sorry for you or anything," Trevor had said almost immediately. It was important to Atticus that Trevor had said that. It had always been important to Atticus that people not feel sorry for him. He saw the way people looked at him. And most times, adults were worse than kids. Real little kids looked at him out of curiosity. They didn't know why he was in a wheelchair and would ask him straight out. And most times, their mothers or fathers would shush them and hurry them away like Atticus was some kind of ghost or something that they should be afraid of.

Where to Begin?

It was the adults who made Atticus feel the worst. They would look at him with a very sad expression, and he would know what they were thinking. They were thinking how sad it was that he would never be able to run or play football or climb a tree.

But Trevor hadn't felt sorry for Atticus. He just wanted to get back at Kevin, he'd said. He didn't want to stand alongside the lockers like everyone else and watch Kevin Thurston act like the big shot. So, in a heartbeat, Trevor pushed through all of Kevin's friends and grabbed the back handles of Atticus's wheelchair. Before anyone knew what was going on, before even Atticus himself had time to react, Trevor was wheeling Atticus down the main hall at blinding speed. After some delay, Atticus could hear Kevin calling after them and could feel the rumbling of their footsteps as Kevin and his cronies thundered down the hall after them. But it was too late. Trevor and Atticus were well out of the school before the door to Mr. Gulf's office ever opened. As they rounded the side of the school, they could hear "KEVIN THURSTON!" and they knew he was done for. Mr. Gulf had no tolerance for "any tomfoolery!" And running in the halls was exactly the kind of thing that could get a guy named Tom or Kevin in trouble.

That was the beginning of Atticus and Trevor's friendship but not the beginning of their adventures. No, that would not come until a little later. That would not come until all of the school was mad at Kevin Thurston and it seemed as if he hadn't a friend in the world.

Looking back, Atticus would never have believed that Kevin Thurston could ever be friendless. Everyone adored him, even teachers—even Molly Vickers.

It stood to reason that Molly Vickers would be crazy about Kevin Thurston. After all, he was the best football player in the school. He was a super jock. He played all the sports and played them better than anyone. He was sure to be a superstar when he entered high school. Molly was the top cheerleader for Walnut Middle School. Not only was she the prettiest girl in school, but she was a great dancer too. She was great in all kinds of sports. Atticus could remember back to the fifth grade when Molly was on the AmeriCheer Dance Squad. She was always flipping and doing cartwheels and making it look so easy to run and dance. Molly was great on her feet.

That was one thing Atticus noticed quite a bit—how people walked. He could always tell kids who weren't so good in sports because when they ran, they kind of kicked their feet out to the side. Their knees would always stay straight in one place while their feet kicked out, making them look clumsy. And when they walked, they came down flat-footed. Atticus had a cousin who never quite picked up her feet enough when she ran. Atticus always winced when he saw her running because it was just a matter of time before she tripped and fell over uneven pavement or a rock or something. But Molly made walking and running look so effortless, and Atticus wished, were he ever to walk, that he would move as she did.

Well, maybe not *exactly* as she did.

There were other reasons he liked to watch her as well. She was pretty. Very pretty. Oh, but he had already mentioned that.

If he were Kevin Thurston, Atticus thought, he would be the happiest guy alive. He would have everything. He would be a great athlete and well liked. He would have the prettiest girl in the whole world always hanging around him and walking to classes with him and cheering him on when he was doing great things on the football field. And, best of all, he would have a nice, normal name. So really, in Atticus's book, there had certainly been no reason for Kevin to act the way he had.

In just recalling those early days, Atticus had to shake his head. It was hard to believe even now that anyone could have done what he did to Molly Vickers. It just didn't make any sense, and never did a girl deserve it less than Molly.

That, Atticus finally realized, had to be the beginning. It had to be when everything began to unravel for Kevin Thurston and when Atticus knew that he must do something to help. Yes, that was the beginning of the end!

★ ★ ★

The
Beginning

★ ★ ★

THE CONTEST

IF there were ever times to be thankful for his wheelchair—and there were very, very few— a pep rally was one of them. While all the kids clambered up the bleachers, finding their own special places in their own special cliques, Atticus always stationed himself in the middle of the bleachers, on the floor, right smack in the middle of all the cheerleaders who were sitting cross-legged on the gym floor with their pom-poms.

Behind him, all the jocks who weren't "in season" picked seats at the highest point in the bleachers. In this case, because it was the fall, the football players were on the gym floor waiting to be announced, while the basketball, soccer, and baseball players sat up at the top of the bleachers. Being ultra-cool wasn't always a matter of looks or clothes. Sometimes it was a seasonal thing, as well.

The behavior of the jocks in the bleachers always mystified Atticus. They acted as though they thought that because they were so high up, none of the teachers would realize that they were the ones who screamed out names at people, hooted and hollered at the cheerleaders, and pitched wadded-up paper balls at the "lesser ones"—the freaks, the geeks, and the outcasts.

The freaks were the kids who experimented with smoking hoping that other kids would think they were cool, when all anyone really thought was that they smelled like smoke. The truth was that they looked ridiculous standing outside in the pouring rain trying to smoke a dampened cigarette. Still, the freaks considered this an act of defiance that made them cool.

The geeks were the kids who were on the honor roll, were in the drama club, and actually liked school. In general, they were pretty good kids, and, by all accounts, Atticus Weaver was a full-fledged geek. Atticus was an excellent student and a member of the chess, debate, and science clubs. Despite that, he was wheelchair-bound, so he was classified as an outcast. The outcast, not to be confused with the freak, was someone who couldn't quite be placed into just one group.

In the case of Trevor Smith, while he was a good athlete, he was also a very good student. And, if that weren't enough, he liked being at school, he never talked back to the teachers, and he didn't cuss or yell. He held open doors for teachers and said things like, "Yes, ma'am," and "No, sir." All of this made him a big-time outcast.

With the jocks all lined up on the top row of the bleachers and the freaks lingering in the middle—where they could join in with the jocks who made fun of the geeks, yet still be far enough away not to be confused with them—this left the front rows to the geeks. Just in case there was a need for a sudden rush to get back to their classrooms, the geeks wanted unobstructed pathways. In fact, the only thing that could trip up the geeks was "the beautiful people," the female version of the jocks, also known as "the beauties." It didn't matter if a beauty had a super-awesome free throw or could score ten goals in ten minutes. The beauties were clean-cut, attractive, well-mannered girls who couldn't be lumped into the same category as the jocks.

Because the beauties and the cheerleaders—often one and the same—all hung out together, they liked to sit down on the front row together. This usually caused great consternation with the geeks, who would begin sweating profusely at the idea that one of the beauties might actually look his or her way.

The remaining group was the outcasts who, because they didn't usually band together very well, were scattered throughout the bleachers, usually looking as though they wished they didn't have to sit with whatever group they were near. Most of the outcasts were invisible to the jocks, freaks, geeks, beauties, and cheerleaders. Atticus Weaver was no exception, even with his cumbersome wheelchair.

So it was easy for Atticus to sit right in the middle of the beauties and the cheerleaders, melt back into his chair, and listen to the conversations that took place. He loved it. He truly loved being able to hear what each girl thought of the jocks, music, teachers, even one another. And being his best buddy and all, Trevor was allowed to sit next to him. The two would bump elbows at the comments the girls made about individual jocks, particularly when there was the very rare but deeply cherished comment that Kevin Thurston thought he was much better than he really was.

But the absolute best thing about sitting there was being so close to Molly Vickers. She was by far the most beautiful girl in school, and, as goofy as this was to think, not just on the outside. She was beautiful on the inside too. She was smart, funny, and nice. She was really nice. When she cheered, she cheered to the geeks and the freaks. She didn't just look up toward the jocks or smile at her beauty friends as most of the other cheerleaders did. She actually looked at the entire student body. And as her eyes roamed the bleachers, she found and actually looked at outcasts. She looked at Trevor. She looked at Atticus. Heart-stopping, pulse-racing stares as they were, she seemed oblivious to her powers. She just shouted, stamped her feet, and cheered for her school.

Her hair was the color of, well, moondust. Atticus thought of moondust because of a particularly embarrassing and goofy song Mrs. Weaver insisted on singing to Atticus over and over again. He had loved it as a child, but, as he tried to point out to his mother, he was no longer a little kid. But she would simply roll her eyes at him and tell him that he would *always* be her baby. And then she would sing.

"On the day that you were born, the angels got together and decided to create a dream come true . . . so they sprinkled moondust in your hair of gold and starlight in your eyes of blue . . . that is why all the girls in town . . . follow you . . . all around. Just like me, they long to be, close to you . . ."

Atticus had the same color hair as Molly Vickers. Only, he thought, hers was much prettier. In fact, just replace the line about girls with *boys*, and he would swear the song had been written just for Molly. He didn't know who sang that original song, but he knew one thing— every boy at Walnut Middle School would follow Molly Vickers anywhere. She had starlight in her eyes of blue. She had beautiful moondust sprinkled in her hair of gold, which had loads of curls that hung down low on her back. She was just . . . perfect.

If anything could distract Atticus Weaver from his studies or bring together the geeks, freaks, and outcasts, it was Molly Vickers.

On this particular day, the pep rally had been postponed until the end of the day. This was because the last time they had had a pep rally, someone had flushed a stink bomb down one of the toilets in the boys' upstairs bathroom, smelling up the entire school. Classes on the second floor actually had to be moved down to the gymnasium because the stench was so powerful. The rest of the day was a joke because no one could concentrate on anything the teachers were saying. Since that time, lots of things had happened in schools around the country with kids doing stupid things for attention. So, thankfully, many schools had adopted a "zero-tolerance policy." Translation— any kid dumb enough to bring anything into school that shouldn't be there would be expelled.

But to be extra safe, Mr. Gulf arranged to have the pep rally held at the end of the day. With everyone present and accounted for on the floor, Mr. Gulf began to introduce the Walnut Middle School football team, one by one. It was no surprise that when Kevin's name was announced, everyone went wild. Everyone, that is, except Trevor and Atticus. Instead, they sat back and watched Molly as she cheered and did a couple of flips. When she did, they were able to see her bloomers, and they snickered to each other. They weren't being weird or anything. That was what the undergarment of the cheerleaders' costume was called—bloomers.

It was what Mr. Gulf talked about next, however, that really caught the boys' attention.

" . . . And the person who sells the most items, earning the most points, will win this brand-new computer," Mr. Gulf said, stepping to the side while his assistant, Mrs. North, pulled a white sheet off the mysterious table next to the podium. Atticus sat up straight in his chair.

A computer! While that wasn't such a big deal to Trevor, it was everything in the world to Atticus. Oh, how he had wanted a computer. There were kids in his class who were turning in assignments they had typed and printed on their computers. They were looking up information on the Internet, never having to leave their houses. The world and all of its information were at their fingertips, and he had been so envious of them all. Why, most of the kids only used their computers for games and emailing junk to one another. For Atticus, it meant endless possibilities.

With his own computer, he could learn everything he needed to know about his disease. And maybe, just maybe, he would be able to find a friend on the Internet who had what he had. Web sites were set up for everything imaginable. He could get more information just sitting in his room than he ever could from his monthly visits to his doctor. Imagine finding someone who understood how he felt, *what* he felt. Trevor was the best friend a guy could have, but still, there were some things that he just didn't understand.

"If you had a computer," Trevor said suddenly, breaking into Atticus's thoughts, "you could get on the Web. We could email each other."

"I'd have to earn more than 750 points. Do you know how many candles and packages of nuts that is?" Atticus replied, playing the pessimist. But Trevor shrugged in a way that was so typical of Trevor. It was one of the reasons Atticus liked him so much. Nothing ever riled him. Nothing ever seemed too hard for him. Nothing ever seemed too far out of reach. It was one of the reasons he was considered an outcast.

"I bet I know a way to make you about 500 points overnight," Trevor said with a gleam in his eye.

"Five hundred points?" Atticus said, raising his eyebrows. Then he laughed. "Yeah, but is it legal?"

"Totally."

While the rest of the school cheered or jeered at Mr. Gulf and his entire speech about school spirit and selling merchandise door-to-door safely, Atticus and Trevor bent their heads down and whispered to each other. While all the cheerleaders yelled and flipped and the beauties cheered and clapped, Trevor shared his idea with Atticus about how he could win a computer. It seemed to Atticus that it wasn't only legal, it was inspired!

This was the beginning, he felt. This was the beginning of so many things. He could hardly wait for the pep rally to end and for school to let out so he could get his hands on the catalog and order form. Maybe that was why he never heard them coming down the bleachers. Maybe that was why he never heard one of the jocks call out to Kevin Thurston, drawing him away from the other players in the middle of the gymnasium floor. Maybe that was why, when he saw the geeks bolt from their seats, he, too, bolted, wanting to be first in line to get an order form.

While he would get no competition from the freaks or the jocks, there were plenty of geeks who wanted to get their hands on *his* computer! If he was going to win a computer, he was going to have to act fast, beating out all the other kids from doing the same thing. Trevor's idea was fresh, but put two or three geek heads together, and they would come up with it soon enough.

The instant Molly and the others gave their final whoop, Atticus lurched forward in his wheelchair, aiming it straight for Mr. Gulf. Instead, he slammed his right wheel into the back of Kevin Thurston, who was slobbering over Molly Vickers and the other beauties.

"Hey!" Kevin jumped. "Idiot. Look where you're going."

"Kevin," one of the beauties pleaded and then smiled down at Atticus in a way that Atticus knew Kevin didn't like.

"You'd think he'd know how to move that thing around by now," Kevin said aloud to no one in particular. A few of the jocks chuckled. "Did ya not see me standing here?"

"He was afraid of being trampled by the geeks," said one of the players.

"No, he was making a rush for the stage," said David Lepac, a sidekick to Kevin. David was dangerously close to repeating the same grade, and the school year had only just begun. That's how stupid he was.

"Oooh, Mr. Gulf," David mimicked Atticus, "how can I be part of the school-spirit drive?"

"Man, how can someone so stupid play football?" a voice piped in. "I'm surprised you can even remember to wear your helmet. Oh, maybe *that's* how it happened." As Trevor spoke, Atticus could see the look of horror come over most of the beauties' faces, while rage swept over both Kevin's and David's faces.

If there was ever any hope that Atticus could steer clear of trouble, Trevor always found a way to put them right in the middle of things. To Trevor, it was just a way of standing up for themselves. It had not escaped Atticus's notice that if someone were picking on Trevor, he would just shrug his shoulders the way he always did.

But were someone to make a remark about Atticus, Trevor was ready to match wits with him—something that most of the jocks were not up for doing.

"Why, you little . . ." Kevin stepped in.

In a flash, Trevor had his hands on the back of Atticus's chair and was ready to move around the pack of jocks.

"Kevin, why don't you just leave them alone?" Molly Vickers said suddenly. Her voice cut through the air like angels' music.

"Yeah," another beauty piped in, and Kevin whirled around toward them. What he was going to say, no one knew. Trevor wasn't going to wait around to find out. In a flash, he jerked Atticus's chair to the side and sideswiped David and Connor Pearson. Before either boy could get ahold of either Atticus or Trevor, Trevor had placed himself and Atticus square in front of Mr. Gulf. As Mr. Gulf happily handed out catalogs, Trevor looked over his shoulder at Kevin and his buddies. But Kevin and his gang were far from Atticus's mind as he got his hands on a catalog and flipped through it. In the middle, next to the order forms, was a picture of the grand prize. It was everything Atticus had ever wanted in a computer. It was top-of-the-line. It was perfect.

"This is exactly what I want, Trev," Atticus said. "It's what I've always wanted." He continued to mutter to himself while staring at the picture. With Trevor pushing him through the school hallways and out the front door, Atticus needn't watch where they were going.

There had been a time when Mrs. Weaver had arranged to have a bus pick up Atticus every day from school. There was a brief overlap of 30 minutes from the time Atticus was out of school to the time she got home from work. In the past, she had arranged for a caregiver to stay with Atticus until she got home. He had absolutely hated it.

It's not that it was Mrs. Thompson's fault or anything. It was her job to make sure that Atticus was safe. He understood that. But it never made things easier to have all the kids see him being lifted in the bus with the special chair elevator lift. It was a big, fat, giant reminder to everyone just how different Atticus was. Forget the name. All anyone had to see was the huge chairlift.

But Trevor had changed all that. He liked pushing Atticus around so much that one day he asked if he could take Atticus home. Living just five blocks from the school, it was easy enough for Trevor to push Atticus home. Instead of Mrs. Thompson staying with him, Trevor stayed. He and Atticus would watch television or just goof off until Mrs. Weaver came home. If ever there were a day when Trevor was sick or couldn't make it, then Mrs. Thompson would be a backup. But that day had never happened. Trevor had always been there for Atticus.

"Hey!" Atticus suddenly looked up from his catalog. "What's the rush?" he asked. Trevor was almost at a run, pushing Atticus's chair very quickly along the uneven sidewalk. Atticus found it increasingly difficult to hold on to his belongings as he was bumped along.

"You trying to kill me?" Atticus called over his shoulder.

"No, but I bet they are," Trevor called back. Without having seen what Trevor was talking about, Atticus's heart sank. He knew. He took a deep breath, leaned forward, and, craning his neck, saw that Kevin Thurston, David Lepac, and Connor Pearson were bearing down on them. They were coming from around the back of the school and running straight for Trevor and Atticus.

"Well, what are you waiting for?" Atticus screamed in a high-pitched voice that was a bit screechier than he would have wished. Panic flooded him. While Kevin Thurston had never actually gotten his hands on Atticus, there was always the fear of it. Kevin and his gang had always threatened, and Atticus had always taken them quite seriously.

He had heard about Kevin. He had heard how Kevin had beaten up a couple of different guys. In fact, he had heard that Kevin got into a huge fight with about ten guys from another school's football team and single-handedly knocked each guy down. David Lepac and Connor Pearson weren't exactly known to be sweethearts, either. With the three of them hot after Trevor and Atticus, the two would surely be in need of an ambulance if Trevor didn't pick up his feet.

"Run!" Atticus screamed over his shoulder, gripping the armrest to his chair.

"I am! I am!"

Trevor pushed forward with renewed urgency, and Atticus could hear his feet hitting the pavement much harder. Never mind that there were tons of kids on the sidewalk. Trevor wheeled them through the crowds, zigzagging around everyone. They were losing time.

"Outta the way! Move! Move!" Trevor began yelling wildly. Atticus could see kids ahead of them turning around to see Trevor and Atticus flying down the sidewalk. Thankfully, everyone stepped off the sidewalk, allowing Trevor to pick up speed.

Again, Atticus braced himself. Not 100 yards away was the end of the sidewalk leading to Walnut Street, the main road. They had one of two choices: keep running straight and risk getting squashed by a car or cut a hard right to stay on the winding sidewalk. With the speed they were traveling compounded by the weight of Atticus's wheelchair, they had another problem to consider—they needed to slow way down or risk flipping over.

Atticus's heart was a heavy and powerful knocking against his chest. Atticus licked his lips. He felt partly frightened and partly excited. This was cutting it a little closer than ever before. Sure, Trevor had mouthed off to Kevin and the guys before. This wasn't the first time they had been chased, but there had always been someone around to save them—Mr. Gulf or another teacher. This time they were off school grounds.

Atticus could also hear Trevor's breathing now. It was labored. Trevor was scared too. He could see the street closing in on them. He was no dummy. He knew they would have to slow down. They couldn't risk running across the street. A thick wall of bushes ran a neat line to the right of them, ending some six feet from the street. There was no way to see if any cars were coming from the right until they actually turned to the right, taking the path. Atticus looked anxiously to their left. No cars, only a dozen or so other kids who had all stopped walking and were now standing in their places watching with open mouths as Trevor pushed on.

Atticus could hear Kevin Thurston calling behind them.

"You might as well give up!" he called out.

"You can't outrun us! Not pushing that heap of junk," another voice called out.

"You're dead!" Connor Pearson called.

They were closing in. It didn't matter how fast Trevor was, pushing the chair slowed him down.

"You see anything from the right?" Trevor called out. His voice sounded strained. Almost panicked.

Atticus knew that if they were caught, Trevor would be the one in danger. There was a question as to what Kevin might do to Atticus, but with Trevor, there was no question at all. Atticus knew it. Trevor knew it.

"What?!" Atticus called back, now gripping the armrests so hard he was afraid he might snap them off.

"To the right! To the right! You see anything?"

"I can't!" Atticus screamed.

A brief frightening thought entered Atticus's mind. Trevor couldn't really be thinking what Atticus feared he was thinking, could he?

Anticipating their next move, Connor Pearson crashed through the wall of bushes. Atticus could hear the commotion and knew they were about to be blocked off from the right. Kevin Thurston and David Lepac were still behind them. And gaining.

With only ten feet to go until the end of the sidewalk, Trevor called out again. The excitement was gone, and pure terror filled Atticus's heart. *He couldn't really be thinking what he was thinking! He couldn't really mean it!*

Atticus saw all the kids standing around, staring. He saw the edge of the sidewalk, that turn to the right that led off toward Walnut Street. He saw the pavement. Walnut Street. He heard the sounds of Trevor's feet slowing, putting on the brakes just before they got to the edge of the road.

Trevor was yelling something at Atticus, but it was all a blur. There was nothing to the left of them. That didn't matter. Only the right mattered. Atticus was straining his eyes to see to the right, praying that Trevor was going to stop in time, digging his hands into the armrests so hard that he would have sworn he was bending the metal.

Suddenly Connor Pearson was to the right of them, arms outstretched like he was going to block them from moving around him and grinning hugely.

Atticus felt the left tire leave the ground, making the chair feel light. It was not a good feeling, and Atticus feared he might get sick. It was an out-of-control feeling he didn't care for at all. He had always trusted Trevor, always. Suddenly, he was uncertain—terrified, to be exact.

"Aha!" Connor pounced forward.

Then, *slam!* The left tire was back on the ground again, hard. And they were cutting back to the left.

"What are you doing?" Atticus screamed.

He jerked his head back to the right again to look for cars. This time he could see. The wall of bushes was gone, and there was nothing obstructing his view. They were at the end of the line, and instead of going right, Trevor had yanked the chair back to the left and was going straight again.

"What are you doing?" Atticus screamed again, stiffening every part of his body.

"We can do it! We can do it!" Trevor called out.

But there was a car coming. Several, in fact.

Then, in what seemed like slow motion, Trevor ran across the street, pushing Atticus out in front of him. Atticus could feel the renewed energy behind the push. He could hear Trevor's feet pounding on the pavement. He could hear his heavy breathing, grunting out as he gave the chair an extra push. But Atticus was unable to appreciate this extra burst of energy. He could only stare to his right, horrified, as a large blue minivan closed in on them. He could see the expression on the face of the poor woman as her mouth formed a perfect O shape. He could see how she flung her arm out as though she were blocking her passenger from some kind of impact, impact on one now-seemingly-small wheelchair. He could hear a girl from somewhere behind them on the lawn of Walnut Middle School scream out. And then, in what had to be a blink of an eye, they were across the street, and all he could hear was the horn honking on the minivan and the tires squealing.

No sooner did they reach the other side of the road than the chair hit the uneven sidewalk. The impact was hard. Atticus could feel Trevor's upper body collapse over the top of the chair. Then, with tremendous force, Atticus was ejected from his seat. Another sickening feeling came over him as he floated through the air. Another eye blink later, he was in a crumpled heap on the grass.

THE COMPUTER

"**ARE** you insane?" Atticus said, rolling over and propping himself up with his arms. He could feel heat against his left cheek and a throbbing sensation in his shoulder. Slowly, he moved his arm in a circular motion and determined it was fine. He wiggled his lower jawbone to make sure it was fine as well and stared hard at Trevor.

Trevor was standing slowly, dusting off his pants and looking sheepishly at Atticus. *That* was not what he had planned. Atticus was sure Trevor had opened his mouth to say as much when they heard another voice.

The blue minivan had pulled over to the side of the road, and a very angry mother-type woman was walking toward them. Atticus knew the look—part fear, part rage.

"Are you boys all right?" she asked as she came closer. Even as she asked, her eyes were on Atticus. He nodded. Trevor busily tipped the wheelchair back onto its wheels and readied to help Atticus back into it. The woman then turned to Trevor.

"What were you thinking?" she shrieked. "You could have killed him!" She waved a hand at Atticus, who was struggling to get back into his seat.

"Yes, ma'am," Trevor said quietly.

"I mean, you could have both been killed flying out like that. I had no way of seeing you. What if I hadn't been paying attention?" she asked. Her voice was much louder than Atticus was sure she intended it to be. "What if I hadn't been able to brake in time? You could have been killed!"

"I'm sorry," Trevor said, more to Atticus than to the woman. And it was clear to Atticus that Trevor felt deeply ashamed. He was unusually pale.

"Why aren't you under adult supervision?" the woman was asking. Her voice was so loud, Atticus couldn't help but cringe. "If your mother knew . . ." Past her, both Atticus and Trevor could see what seemed like a hundred kids standing out on the lawn of the school watching them. The woman's voice was echoing all over Walnut Street.

Once Atticus was in his chair, Trevor leaned over him.

"I'm sorry, buddy," he said. His voice was in a hushed tone. "I really thought . . . I wouldn't have ever . . . man, I'm so sorry."

"You can't just go peeling out like that. You have to stay on the sidewalk," the woman was saying. Still frightened herself, she was babbling.

"It's okay," Atticus breathed finally. "At least we got away from them." He nodded across the street. Trevor turned to see Kevin Thurston, Connor Pearson, and David Lepac all standing close together, each one thumping a fist into a hand. *We'll get you later*, they seemed to be saying.

"I'm sorry, Atticus," Trevor began to stammer. "I'll never let you down like that again. I swear it."

"Well, I want your mother's telephone number," the woman said, suddenly jarring the boys back to what she was talking about. "I just don't think she would be very happy to know this is the way you boys behave. And you," she said, waving a finger at Trevor, "his life depended on you making the right decision."

Atticus felt a new wave of panic come over him. Having Trevor as a best friend was the best thing that had ever happened to Atticus. If his mother were to find out what a close call they'd just had, she would never let Trevor push him again. It would be Mrs. Thompson and the huge chairlift all the time. Atticus just couldn't bear the thought of that. Having Trevor escort him home wasn't like having supervision. Even though he knew that Trevor was there to make sure he didn't fall or anything like that, it was just like having a friend over, and it gave Atticus a feeling of independence.

Trevor had made a mistake, and he felt really bad about it. It was true that it was a stupid thing to do, but Atticus knew that Trevor had panicked. He had been panicked too.

"I mean, what would make you do something like that?" the exasperated woman asked.

"Them." Trevor pushed his chin forward, pointing with it instead of his finger. The woman turned to look over her shoulder at David Lepac, Connor Pearson, and Kevin Thurston. As soon as she looked at them, they shrank away, disappearing behind the wall of bushes.

"They were chasing *you*?" she asked in disbelief. "What for?"

"To beat us up," Trevor answered honestly. The woman looked astonished.

"*Both* of you?" she asked again. She did not look directly at Atticus, but it was clear what she was thinking. *You never hit a kid with glasses, and you never, never hit a kid in a wheelchair.* Atticus Weaver had both. While he might have had hair of gold and moondust like Molly Vickers, it was the only thing he had that was worth bragging about. At least in his mind. He was too pale, too skinny. His ears were a little too big. He wore glasses, and he had to get around in a wheelchair. Still, this poor woman could not believe that anyone in his or her right mind would ever pick on a kid like Atticus Weaver. She looked over her shoulder again toward the direction of Kevin Thurston and his friends, but they were gone from sight.

"Yes, ma'am," Trevor answered up again. While he spoke, Atticus busily secured himself back into the seat and turned around in his chair, checking the backpack. Behind his seat was a neat little backpack that carried all of his books. Everything was still in place.

"Well, I . . ." Her voice trailed off. For just a moment, she was speechless.

Trevor took this opportunity to soften her up. Maybe if she felt sorry for them, she could forgive Trevor for almost killing them all.

"You see, that was why I ran like I did. I tried to make that turn," he said, waving a finger at the sidewalk where it turned off sharply at the edge of the bushes. "I was trying to make it, but this one guy jumped out at us. It scared me, and I turned the chair and went right into the street. I wouldn't have ever done that on purpose. I didn't mean to scare you. I didn't mean to scare us!"

She was nodding slowly, understanding.

"We'd better get going," Atticus said meekly. "I need to take my heart medicine."

Trevor whipped his head around toward Atticus. The woman's mouth fell open.

"Oh," she stammered.

Atticus gave a weak cough into his fisted hand.

"Oh, yes," Trevor said, hustling behind Atticus's chair and pushing it back onto the sidewalk. "We'd better hurry. Thank you for stopping, ma'am. You scared those guys off. Thanks a lot!" And before another word could be uttered, before the woman could insist on getting a telephone number from the boys, they were rushing home.

The Computer

Neither boy spoke to the other until they had turned off Walnut Street and made their way down Spring Road. Still, the question drummed through Atticus's mind. What would they have done if Kevin and the others had caught them? Would it have been more than a pushing and shoving match? Would they have only harassed Trevor, or would someone have pushed Atticus as well? He licked his lips and realized how very dry his mouth was.

"Hey, Trev," Atticus thought out loud. "You think they would really, ya know, hit us?"

"What? Are you kidding me?" Trevor laughed back at this. "They've been waiting to get us for a long time."

"Yeah." Atticus thought about this. It was true. There had been plenty of times Kevin and his buddies had come close to getting Trevor and Atticus, but they had always managed to get away. That must have caused a lot of frustration for those guys. "But, do ya think . . . ?"

"Do I think they would punch you out even though you're in a wheelchair?"

Trevor cut right to it—again, one of the things Atticus really liked about him. He didn't pretend not to notice that Atticus was in a wheelchair. He didn't act as if Atticus could do

45

the same things he could. In fact, the first time they met, Trevor Smith didn't save Atticus from Kevin Thurston because it bothered him that a bunch of guys were picking on a kid in a wheelchair. He just did it because it would bother Kevin. He did it because he would have done that for anyone. Even a kid in a wheelchair.

"Yeah, I think he's mean enough that he would just as soon punch you in the face as look at you. That what you mean?"

"Yeah," Atticus answered and settled back into his seat. He could have pushed himself. In his backpack was a strong set of gloves. But lately, he rarely used them. It was just easier to talk and do things if Trevor pushed. And Trevor seemed to like pushing.

"I'm in training for the U.S. bobsled team," he liked to say.

So Atticus just settled back and let Trevor move them along.

It was hard to explain, but Atticus kind of liked the idea that Kevin Thurston would punch his lights out. Imagine the talk at school if Atticus came in sporting a shiner. Imagine what his mother would say if she saw that he had a black eye! He squirmed in his chair again.

"You ever been punched?" Atticus asked Trevor.

They moved past another house before Trevor answered.

"You afraid of getting hit?" he asked.

"I'm just wondering, is all. You ever been punched?"

"Yeah, plenty of times by my brother," he said. Atticus frowned at this. While he didn't have any siblings of his own and had no idea what a pain it was to have to share things with a brother or sister, this just didn't seem the same to him.

"That isn't the same, is it?"

"Tell that to Joe," Trevor laughed, but it wasn't a happy kind of laugh. "Man, he pounds me into dust sometimes."

"He ever give you a black eye?" Atticus asked, now more interested.

"Well, no. Not a black eye. My mom would kill him if he ever did that. He knows it too. But he's done stuff like shove me in a closet or stuff my head in a trash can. Once he duct-taped me to our tree out back and turned the sprinkler on me. My mom was real mad about that."

"But you haven't ever gotten a black eye?" Atticus persisted. Finally Trevor conceded. "No, nothing like that."

They had pushed passed several streets, including Atticus's, but he said nothing. It wasn't that he hadn't noticed. He had. He knew they were going to Trevor's house. And as soon as they got inside, Atticus knew he would need to page his mother on her beeper to let her know where he was. Until then, he would worry about what it felt like to be punched. He wondered what Molly Vickers would say if she saw him wearing a black eye. It would be like a badge of honor. It would be a sign to every kid who was ever afraid of Kevin Thurston or a bully like him that getting punched wasn't so bad. He imagined that it would hurt initially, but that would be it. After that, it would be up to him how he would handle the actual black eye. He could act ashamed of it, or he could wear it proudly. He would wear it proudly. It would be his own way of showing everyone that he wasn't afraid of standing up to Kevin and his gang. He could have been like the others and always said, "Oh, Kevin, you're so great. You're such a jock!" He could do all that. Or, he could say what he wanted to say. He could say things like, "Hey, Kevin, you've got the brains of a hamster!"

Never, in Atticus's mind, was an event ever so greatly anticipated as the eventual, inevitable showdown between him and Kevin Thurston.

When he was little, it had been Santa Claus. Most recently, there was the big deal of him getting a new remote-controlled chair in his house that moved up and down the staircase on an escalatorlike contraption. That really was a big deal. But this was different.

There was no chance that Santa Claus was going to turn violent or that one of the elves was going to leap out of the sled and beat him up. The inevitable, custom-made punch in the eye from Kevin Thurston was far more exciting to think about. It was nerve-racking, sure. Santa Claus is a scheduled event. You know when he's coming, and he's really nice about it. There was just no telling when Kevin Thurston would finally get his hands on Atticus. And there was no way of knowing exactly what he was going to do to Atticus when he caught him. To this, Atticus had given a great deal of thought. Would Kevin rough him up, punch him in the eye, or break his bones? What would he do? No one knew.

There was the thrill of getting away. Never before had Atticus known such excitement. And while he didn't know what it felt like to actually run, he could now imagine!

There was so much more. Before, being an outcast, no one ever took any notice of him. No one cared what he did. He was the kid who usually got the only A in class. He was the guy who knew all the answers and the guy the teacher would finally call on after everyone else had flubbed the answer. Now, however, he was part of something much more exciting, and people were talking about it. It was exciting and dangerous. He could have told his mother about it. He could have told Mr. Gulf, the principal, about it and have Kevin Thurston warned, but he hadn't, and he wouldn't. He wasn't afraid of a black eye. He wasn't afraid of being hurt. He liked to think that he was making a stand for all the outcasts, all the geeks, maybe even the freaks. He liked to think that he was part of something brave and that maybe when people talked about the Atticus/Kevin showdown, they would talk about how brave he had been. Maybe even Molly Vickers.

"Okay, lock down." Atticus heard Trevor's voice and suddenly realized he had not been paying attention to Trevor at all. Atticus was sitting outside Trevor's house at the crest of the driveway just outside the garage door. There was a slight hill, so to be careful, Trevor had wanted Atticus to flip down the brakes on his chair. "I'll be right back," Trevor said and hurried off to the front door.

Once inside, Trevor ran through the house and unlocked the garage door from the inside so that he and Atticus could go through the garage into the house. To get to the front door was far too difficult as it had seven steps up to the porch. Instead, they could go through the garage and only have to make one little step inside the kitchen.

Ten seconds after he had disappeared, Atticus could hear Trevor opening the garage door. It was barely two feet off the ground when he ducked beneath it and came out smiling. He had an embarrassed look on his face.

"Hey," he said, "I am sorry about, you know, what happened earlier." Like Atticus, he had been thinking about things himself.

"Connor jumped out at us," Atticus said Trevor stepped out onto the driveway and walked around behind Atticus's wheelchair. "What else could you do?" Atticus went on, trying to make his friend feel better.

"Well, not *that*," Trevor mused. "I won't do it again."

He pushed Atticus in through the garage and bumped the chair up over the small step into the kitchen. Neither one of them spoke of "the incident" again. After calling Mrs. Weaver, they made themselves a little snack of peanut butter sandwiches, potato chips, two Twix bars apiece, a banana for Atticus, and a bowl of Fruit Loops (without milk) for Trevor while they waited for the popcorn to pop. They did, after all, burn quite a few calories in their jog-for-life from Kevin Thurston and company. There was no way either one of them could even begin to think about computers and catalog sales until they were replenished.

Balancing the large popcorn bowl in his lap, Atticus wheeled himself into the office of the Smith house while Trevor turned on the computer. The Smith house was the near-perfect setup for Atticus. Actually, he had only been inside Trevor's bedroom one time. Because it was upstairs, Mr. Smith had had to carry Atticus up the stairs. But the office, which had the computer and video game equipment, and the family room were on the first floor. Excluding Trevor's bedroom, the first floor had everything they needed. And it was there that the two friends came up with the greatest catalog-selling scheme that any two students from Walnut Middle School had ever devised.

It just so happened that Mr. Smith ran an advertising agency.

The Computer

"He checks his email like every 30 minutes," Trevor said over his shoulder. While he logged on, Atticus examined some of the popcorn kernels at the bottom of the bowl. He liked the kernels that started to pop but didn't quite make it. He would pop these into his mouth and crunch away. Trevor didn't mind the fact that it meant that Atticus had to stick his hand all the way into the popcorn bowl to find the half-popped kernels. In return, this was Atticus's way of being polite and not looking at Trevor while he logged on. Best friends that they were, they never shared nor asked each other secret or personal information like passwords, combinations, or what embarrassing songs their moms sang. Atticus was quite sure no one would ever guess his password for the school computers, as no one in the ninth grade had ever read *To Kill a Mockingbird*. How many Boo Radleys could there be?

"Okay," Trevor said. Within 30 minutes they were able to design their own Web site, describing all the items they wanted to sell, including a price list. They also scanned pictures from the catalog and uploaded them to the site.

It was good. It looked as professional as anything they had seen on the Internet, but Trevor frowned and leaned back into his father's chair.

"We need a hook," he said. "That's how my dad would say it. Something that makes us different from any other kid trying to sell this stuff." He picked up the catalog, examined it for a moment, and then let it fall to the desk. "We need a hook," he said again, muttering into the computer's monitor. "We need a hook."

There had been a very awkward moment in Mrs. Baker's class several weeks ago when she was talking to the class about the different strains of plants. Atticus believed she had an unnatural fixation with tomatoes. "Paradise's lost fruit" she called them, and she talked about the darn things all the time. It wasn't like they were Three Musketeers bars or anything. Still, she had forced the class to listen to her while she lectured on the tomato and all the different strains of it. She was trying to point out how horticulturists identified different varieties when she called a group of boys to the front of the class. She had six boys standing (or in Atticus's case, sitting) for the rest of the class to examine. Then she said, "Let's put them into categories, eliminating the strains that are different."

Billy Watson, Connor Pearson, Gerald Boyles, Brian Gable, and Atticus Weaver were all wearing T-shirts, while Martin Franks was wearing a button-down shirt.

"Good," Mrs. Baker had said. Martin sat down. "Now, let's go through again."

Everyone identified that Connor Pearson was wearing a baseball cap. He sat down. Everyone was wearing blue jeans except Billy Watson, who was wearing some kind of dress pants his mother had probably made him wear because he looked particularly pained when this was identified out loud. That left Brian, Atticus, and Gerald Boyles. What was so obvious and had been from the very beginning was that there had been five boys standing and one sitting. But no one wanted to identify it out loud, and so every person pretended not to notice.

"What else?" Mrs. Baker urged the class, wanting desperately to get on with her lesson about the tomato—Paradise's lost fruit. Atticus sighed heavily.

"Well," Nicki Coleman spoke up. "Brian has dark hair, and Atticus and Gerry have light hair."

"Very good," Mrs. Baker said.

Atticus had had enough.

"Or, one kid can't walk and is in a wheelchair, and the other two can and aren't. No, wait. Everyone else can."

Mrs. Baker looked grief-stricken, as did the entire class. Atticus could see people shifting uncomfortably in their chairs. Had Trevor been in his class, Atticus was sure he would have spoken up. He was the only *real* person in Atticus's life besides his mom.

It had been a stupid exercise. Atticus wheeled himself back to his desk, not bothering to look at anyone else. What? Were they afraid they would've hurt his feelings if they had identified him as the first variety of a tomato? Did they think he didn't realize that he was in a chair? Did they think he didn't know that?

Atticus looked up from his popcorn bowl again and found Trevor grinning at him.

"What?"

"I have it," Trevor said slowly. "That is, if you don't care."

"About what?" Atticus asked, rolling forward a bit so that he could see what Trevor was typing.

Trevor had found the hook. He identified Atticus as a tomato right away.

"Child in wheelchair needs your help!" Trevor typed happily along. He went on to describe the desperate need for a new computer so that this poor wheelchair-ridden kid could have access to the Internet. He wrote that by ordering the variety of catalog items offered, a new world would be opened for Atticus. Orders could be placed through the Smith Advertising Agency with a check or money order. No cash please.

Atticus and Trevor smiled at their work.

With several more clicks, they sent off the email with the link to their Web site to the long list of every human being they could think of, including Mrs. Weaver's colleagues at the local hospital.

"I bet we'll get about 100," Trevor nodded to himself. "I'll bet we'll get like 200 and not even have to leave the house!"

• • • •

It was 367 to be exact. And most people ordered several items. The response was overwhelming.

Once the email was circulated around St. Ann's Hospital, Atticus and his mom quickly discovered how caring and charitable most people can be. In fact, there came a time when Mrs. Weaver began telling people they were no longer taking orders because Atticus had to turn in his order sheets.

Atticus and Trevor waited until the very last day to turn in their orders to Mr. Gulf. And they waited until after school. They kept their success top-secret, not letting anyone know how many orders they had placed. It took a thick binder to hold all the checks and paperwork.

And just like the boys, Mr. Gulf was sure this would be the winning entry.

"Go take a look at the computer, Mr. Weaver," Mr. Gulf said to Atticus, "as I believe you are going to be its new owner."

Trevor could hear Atticus breathing heavily as they paid a visit to the beautiful computer (and accessories) in Mr. Gulf's office.

"I can't wait," Atticus said, running his fingers over the keyboard.

"We got a couple of weeks before we find out," Trevor reminded him. "It will take a while to go through everyone's orders."

"I can't wait," Atticus said again under his breath. "I just can't wait."

THE ANNOUNCEMENT

THE beginning . . . It was hard for Atticus to really say what the actual beginning was. It had seemed that the beginning had to be when Trevor and Atticus joined forces against Kevin Thurston. But as he moved through the story, Atticus realized that the actual beginning was probably the day of the announcement.

It was all mixed up together. Because even as he identified the beginning as the day of the announcement, it was hard to say *which* announcement. Was it the announcement that Atticus had indeed won the computer, outselling any other student in Walnut Middle School history? Or was it the announcement that Molly Vickers, the queen of the beauties and the cheerleaders, was trying out for the football team as kicker?

To the other students of Walnut Middle School, it was not earth-shattering news that Atticus Weaver had won the contest. It wasn't even news. To all the kids who either pretended not to notice he was in a wheelchair for fear of hurting his feelings or had categorized him as an outcast *because* he was in a wheelchair, no one seemed to think it was any big deal. For all they knew, he had actually wheeled himself around to more than 400 different houses.

Instead, what Atticus heard was a lot of "It figures" when his name was announced as the winner. As near as he could tell, he and Trevor were the only ones who cared. Everyone else was far too busy talking about the other announcement—the *real* announcement.

Molly Vickers was trying out for the football team to replace Brian McPhearson, who broke his ankle in football practice. Brian was a soccer player and the football team's only kicker. So when the coach announced he would be holding tryouts for a new kicker, there had been talk of some soccer players trying out. That wasn't news. But no one had expected a girl soccer player, a beauty, to go for it. And no one, but no one, would have ever believed that Molly Vickers would make such an attempt.

More than anything, Atticus wanted to get his computer home and set it up. He couldn't wait to get everything installed so that he could set up his very own Internet account. Trevor would be the very first person he would email.

But there was really never any question as to what Atticus and Trevor *had* to do. They had to join the rest of the freaks, geeks, outcasts, beauties, cheerleaders, and jocks who were going to the tryouts to watch Walnut Middle School history being made.

With the ring of the final bell, Atticus hurried to Mr. Gulf's office to inspect his new computer and place a call to his mother, begging her to come directly to the school to pick up his computer while he watched the lovely Molly Vickers try out. Well, he didn't tell his mother Molly was lovely. That bit of information he kept to himself.

With his computer under lock and key and the promise that his mother would safely deliver it home, Atticus headed out to the field behind the school. There was a nervous chatter that echoed up and down the halls as kids put away their books and notebooks and prepared to watch a little football.

"What's she trying to prove?" someone asked.

"I heard she's been practicing all summer," another said.

"She just wants to be closer to Kevin Thurston," someone suggested, and it was all Atticus could do to keep from turning around and saying something. It was at that point Trevor took over the chair and began pushing them past everyone, racing out to the field. But before they could make it outside, Trevor and Atticus heard someone else say, "Boy, I bet Kevin doesn't like this at all!"

In fact, the more people they passed, the more they heard speculation about the relationship between Molly and Kevin and how this tryout (and the possibility of her making the team) could affect it. As they reached the field, Gerald Boyles summed it up for most of the jocks when he said, "I don't know what everyone is getting so upset about. She's not going to make it. She's a girl. And she's little. She's not going to make it."

Even if someone were going to respond to that statement, it would have been drowned out by the sudden cheering (and jeering) as the football team, including the new hopefuls, came out from the locker room area. They came jogging out toward the field, ignoring the crowds, focusing on the field only. There were 11 people trying out for the new kicker position—ten boys and one Molly Vickers.

Molly looked the most nervous by far, Atticus decided. Her normally flawless face was tight and anxious-looking. Usually she was smiling and talking to people—any people, no matter the person, no matter the category. But today she was tuning everyone out. She didn't want to look at anyone, and it was clear that she just wished everyone would go away. Had this been an attempt to simply get attention, as someone had suggested earlier, it was clear she had changed her mind. Besides, Atticus didn't believe that anyway. She got plenty of attention as a cheerleader and a beauty. She was the best girl soccer player Walnut Middle School had. And while Atticus had never seen her play himself, he had heard she was also an awesome softball player.

As the kickers stepped out onto the field, Atticus felt a knot form in his stomach. He was nervous for her. Kids were piling into the bleachers, finding their spots. The out-of-season jocks headed for the top, while the few geeks who decided to stick around for the show lingered at the bottom, as far away from the jocks as possible. The freaks and the outcasts were sprinkled throughout, most not even bothering to go to the bleachers. Instead, they hung around the outskirts of the field, feigning disinterest. Only the beauties and fellow cheerleaders hovered as closely as Coach Powell would allow.

Any condescending remarks were drowned out by Molly's supportive friends. There was no way that the obnoxious mouth of Gerald Boyles was going to be heard over the cheers of Amy Loe. She had a louder voice than all the other cheerleaders put together. So while Molly nervously warmed up, doing a variety of stretches, Amy loudly coached her from the sidelines, much to the irritation of Coach Powell. He just wanted to replace his kicker. Instead, he had a turnout that he normally didn't even see for a scheduled football game.

"All right! Let's get this show on the road so we can let some of these circus freaks go home!" Coach Powell blew his whistle. The crowd heckled him.

He ran down the list of names he had on his clipboard, checking off each person as they called out, "Here." When he called out the last alphabetized name, Vickers, there was a loud cheer from the stands. Coach Powell was unmoved.

The tryouts began as a normal football practice, with Coach Powell leading the team in exercises. They jogged laps and performed calisthenics like jumping jacks and bear crawls. Then they were divided into groups, with the assistant coaches taking one group for hitting drills and another for catching and running drills. Atticus watched them with mild interest while the kickers all stood around, nervously chatting among themselves. Only, no one was talking to Molly. She stood off to the side, staring down at her shoes. Only when the coach called out to everyone trying out did she raise her head and trot over toward him.

Amy Loe was screaming at the top of her lungs.

"Whoo! Go Molly! Whoo! Moll—eeee! Whoo!"

Coach Powell, who was about to speak to the new recruits, turned and stared at Amy for several seconds. He opened his mouth to say something and then snapped it shut. He shook his head, looked back at his clipboard, and sighed.

"All right! Let's just get this going." He spoke loudly so everyone could hear him. Then, for added effect, he looked over to Amy Loe to make sure she was okay with that. She was.

Each kicker was given six opportunities to kick the ball through the uprights while Coach Powell made notations on his clipboard. Of the 11 people trying out, 7 of the kickers made every goal. Then each kicker had to kick several goals as though it were a real game. Once the snap was made, the offensive line charged forward, rushing the kicker.

Trevor leaned over to Atticus when Molly's name was called. "They want to see if she freaks out."

Because the coach was moving the tryouts in alphabetical order, everyone in the stands had been allowed to watch the ten male kickers go before Molly Vickers. And everyone in the stands had seen that, of the ten kickers, only four hadn't completely panicked when the linesmen rushed forward, yelling. Only four had been able to kick the ball and score. But none of the kickers was ever actually touched. It was, Atticus could see, all psychological—something that Molly Vickers was used to. She knew firsthand as a cheerleader the effects of people shouting out and calling names. So when the coach called out her name, she seemed unmoved by the chaos it created.

"Moll—eee! Whoo-hoo! Go, Molly, bab—eee! Whoo!"

Coach Powell shot another look at Amy Loe.

Molly positioned herself in the field, shaking her feet and loosening up her muscles. She seemed completely oblivious to the calls of her friends. She was focused. She was ready. She had already proven she could kick the ball very hard and very far through the uprights. Still, the crowd became extremely quiet as they watched how she would react to the pressure of the linesmen.

It was David Lepac who called for the snap of the ball. He was to act as Molly's guard, stopping the line from coming in and tackling her. But instead of protecting her as he had done with the ten boys, he stepped away as soon as the ball was snapped.

Connor Pearson was able to rush in easily enough. Jeff Borden, T. J. Savage, and Cameron Norris all rushed in as well, and Molly was never able to kick. There was a sudden chorus of boos and hisses from the cheerleaders. Faintly, from the top row of the bleachers came some cheers. More boos followed this, with all the beauties and cheerleaders facing the jocks.

"What's this?" Coach Powell demanded. "What's going on?"

Most of the players only looked down at the ground, slowly moving back to their positions on the field. Atticus could see that a handful of players had actually tried to hold the rushing line, but without the support of David Lepac and some of the others, it had been impossible.

Someone muttered a response to the coach. It was obviously an answer he did not like. He began shaking his head furiously, pointing to various players on the field.

"We're going to try this again, and this time we're going to ACT LIKE FOOTBALL PLAYERS!" he shouted at the team. Only David Lepac was watching the coach. Every other player was busily looking to the ground for something that was never destined to be found so that he would not have to meet the angry eye of his coach.

"Whoo! Moll—eee! Whoo! Don't let them rattle you, Molly! You can do this, Mol! You're better than they are! Whoo!"

Coach Powell's shoulders dropped again, and Atticus could see that his patience with everyone was running out. David Lepac was back on the line, ready to snap the ball to Jeremy Thomas, who was supposed to catch and hold the ball for Molly to kick. Atticus watched David carefully. He was down in a three-point stance, one hand resting on his thigh while the other rested on his knuckles on the ground. From this crouching position, he was looking up and talking directly to T. J. Savage and Jeff Borden. It was subtle, but there was a nod of the head with Jeff Borden. Kevin Thurston kept his head down as though he were concentrating on the next play.

Coach Powell blew the whistle.

Amy Loe yelled so loud, the sounds of the football players grunting and yelling couldn't be heard.

For a moment, there seemed to be an effort by Molly's line to hold the other side off. Then the entire wall opened up. Again, T. J. Savage, Jeff Borden, and Cameron Norris came crashing through. They stormed forward, running Jeremy Thomas over. Still, the ball had been snapped and kicked.

"WHOOOO! OH, YEAH! I KNEW YOU COULD DO IT, BAB—EEEEEE!" Amy screamed and jumped around, leading everyone in the stands in a victory cheer.

Molly had made the kick, but she had also been sacked. Lying on the ground, she was a little dazed and probably never heard how wild the crowd went.

Coach Powell blew the whistle.

"WHOO, MOLL—EEEEEEE! I KNEW YOU COULD! DO IT AGAIN, MOL! OH, YEAH, BABY!"

"Amy, please." Coach Powell turned to her, and she suddenly quieted down, looking rather embarrassed. Slowly, Molly got to her feet, smiling sheepishly at Amy.

"That was a fine kick, Molly," the coach told

her. He turned to the team. "Now, I don't know what you boys are thinking. Could it be that you're really tired? You just couldn't hold the brute force of Norris, Savage, and Borden?" There were a few chuckles. "Maybe we need to do more strength and conditioning training." This suggestion, however, was met with loud groans.

Coach Powell ignored this and turned back to all the kickers. "As you know, there will be two picks. And I have to tell you it won't be easy because you all did really well. I didn't realize what great talent we have here. But there can only be two. I'll have the new team roster posted outside my office at the end of practice."

With that, he called for the entire team to run laps. Molly and the other kickers ran along as well while Coach Powell went over to have a discussion of some kind with the other coaches, presumably about the kickers. People in the stands began to leave, all loudly discussing what they thought of the tryouts.

"You think she made it?" Atticus asked over his shoulder, not breaking eye contact from the coaches.

"I don't know. She's got the best kick," Trevor said thoughtfully. "And she's the only one who had to kick under pressure like that and still score."

Atticus found Molly in the midst of all the other football players. She was easy enough to find. She was the smallest one out there with a blonde ponytail streaming along behind her. Only Carlos Munoz was as small as Molly, but he didn't have a ponytail. Both Carlos and Molly were up toward the front of the pack, beating out most of the team while they sprinted along the track. Because of her soccer background, Molly was used to running.

"Yeah," Atticus said, still not taking his eyes from the field, "but she's a girl." He wasn't sure that kicking under pressure would be enough to let her make the team. "Some people don't like the idea of a girl playing on the team."

"Coach doesn't care about that," Trevor piped in. "He just wants to win."

• • • •

But he certainly didn't win any friends. At least, not with Kevin Thurston's crowd. As promised, the new roster for the Walnut Middle School football team was posted at the end of practice, and Molly Vickers was listed as the school's new kicker. Steve Carter also made the cut, acting as second-string.

It was all Atticus heard about for days. But as much as Atticus liked Molly, he had other

71

things to think about—specifically, his computer.

The same evening Molly Vickers made Walnut Middle School history, Atticus and Trevor were able to set up his grand-prize computer. Before the night was over, Atticus and Trevor were instant messaging each other. Since Trevor had been with him when they collected all the checks from Mr. Smith and when Atticus was announced to be the winner, there really wasn't much to talk about online *except* Molly.

Mostly, they were having fun communicating with each other late into the night. It hadn't really mattered what they were talking about. It was funny, however, that a seemingly pointless conversation over the computer would later prove to be so important. They had been talking about how great Molly was and what jerks Kevin Thurston, Cameron Norris, Connor Pearson, and the others were when Trevor shared new gossip Atticus had not yet heard.

TSJr4: You could tell they were doing it on purpose.

Aticus8: You know who started it? It was Kevin. I know it.

TSJr4: Yeah, did you see how he acted like he didn't know what was going on when the coach yelled at everyone?

Aticus8: Yeah, he wasn't fooling anyone. I bet he made them do it.

TSJr4: I heard that Molly doesn't like Kevin anymore.

Aticus8: Really?

Atticus reread this entry, hoping it didn't sound too happy. It was no secret that Atticus liked Molly. Practically every boy did. But he didn't want to be too obvious to Trevor. Trevor really didn't care too much about any of the girls in school. Oh, he noticed them all right. He just didn't talk about any one particular girl. He cared more about sports and computers.

TSJr4: Someone told her that Kevin told those guys to make sure she didn't make a goal. So she asked Kyle Patrick if it was true, but he said he didn't know what she was talking about. But she could tell he was lying. Amy Loe talked to some of the other players, and they said something different.

Aticus8: Like who?

TSJr4: I don't know. Cheerleaders and football players were talking about it. You know how they all hang together.

Aticus8: And Amy heard about this?

TSJr4: Yeah. They told Amy that Kevin told them to make it hard for Molly to be able to kick the ball. You know what that means.

Aticus8: Then she wouldn't look so good.

TSJr4: Yeah, he'd do anything to keep her off the team. That's what I heard. But I also heard that the guys on the team are fighting with one another now.

Aticus8: About what?

TSJr4: Some of the guys said they wanted Molly on the team 'cause she was good and they didn't care if she was a girl. But some others said they wouldn't play if there was a girl on the team.

Aticus8: That's stupid.

TSJr4: Kevin Thurston said his dad said he wouldn't let his son play with a girl. And Cameron Norris and Connor Pearson said the same thing.

Aticus8: So, who cares? It's not like this is college ball and we're playing for a national title, anyway. No one cares about this football team.

It was true. It wasn't like there was a chance that this team could even go to a state championship game. Walnut Middle School was only one of about eight middle schools in the area that even had a football team. So before the season was out, Walnut Middle School played the same teams over and over again. Maybe, though Atticus wasn't sure, there was a trophy given out to all the players just for trying.

TSJr4: People care enough that they're saying she ought to quit.

Aticus8: She was the best kicker. I think she should stay.

TSJr4: Maybe you're just saying that because you like her.

Atticus flinched. It was true. He couldn't deny it, but he was embarrassed by it. Molly Vickers didn't even know he was alive. She was nice to him just like she was nice to everyone. But she probably didn't even know his last name. Atticus decided to ignore that comment.

Aticus8: The only people who are mad about it are the guys she beat out of a kicking position or Kevin and his stupid friends.

TSJr4: Yeah, and some of the cheerleaders.

Aticus8: What about them?

TSJr4: I hear some of them don't think she should be on the football team, either. Parents too. I guess there are a lot of people who don't like the idea of her playing football.

The door to Atticus's room cracked open, and Mrs. Weaver poked her head in.

"It's late," she said. "You need to sign off."

Atticus nodded and typed good-bye to Trevor. But even as he went to bed, he couldn't help thinking how stupid it all was to not let Molly play. It was something he dreamed about all the time. It was something that he wished he could do. And to not let Molly play because she was a girl was stupid. She was just as big as Carlos Munoz, and no one questioned whether he should play or not.

It was hard to see then, but Atticus later realized that this was the beginning of the conflict. The very conflict that led to the beginning of everything.

★ ★ ★

The
Conflict

★ ★ ★

THE FIGHT

IF Molly Vickers entertained any ideas that being on the football team would make her more popular, she was right about that. It was all anyone could talk about. Whether they thought she should be on the team or not, Molly Vickers was the name on everyone's lips. The local newspaper did a story on her, even taking her picture holding a football in her arms outside the school. She was quoted as saying she hoped to be a strong addition to the team.

Coach Powell made a statement as well, saying pretty much the same thing. But no other football players would say anything to the press. No one except Kevin Thurston himself. He told the reporter that he thought it was going to cause a lot of problems. He was afraid that the Cougars' offensive line would have to work twice as hard to protect the kicker *because* she was a girl. He was afraid more attention was going to be paid to the fact that she was a girl than to how good a player she was or the overall team was.

He couldn't have been more right, and Atticus wondered if Molly wished she had never tried out for the team.

Monday started off with a bang. Someone had taken the picture from the newspaper article and drawn things all over it. It was safe to say that the drawings were bad and Molly's feelings were really hurt. The picture was taped up over her locker so everyone could see it. Molly had to clamber on top of the row of lockers to pull it down. By that time, everyone in the entire school was watching, and most were laughing. Even if Atticus hadn't already disliked Kevin Thurston, his feelings would still have turned into a full-fledged hate by the end of the day.

Teachers had a difficult time controlling the kids. There were Molly jokes being told in class. And this Molly situation had created the opportunity for the freaks to make remarks to the jocks. By mid-afternoon there were two different fights in which five different kids were suspended from school. It was crazy. Who would have thought that one girl, who everyone always liked before she became a football player, could stir up such trouble?

But that wasn't the worst of it. There was something far worse that happened than just scribbled lines on a picture. There were threats made against Molly that no one thought were funny. And if whoever wrote it meant for it to be funny, he or she was very wrong. There had been enough bad things happening in schools. You weren't supposed to joke around about things like guns and bombs. You just didn't say dumb things like that.

That was something that Atticus didn't understand. When those things happened, the press talked about it over and over again, and the kids who had done the bad things got their names mentioned. It was the very thing, it seemed to Atticus, they had wanted. To Atticus, it was like those stupid KKK people on television talk shows. They would dress up in their ridiculous white robes, go on a talk show, and get in shouting matches with members of the audience. By looking at them, it was clear to Atticus that these people didn't or couldn't get attention in any other way. It seemed reasonable to think, then, that if no one paid them any attention, they would figure out something else to do with themselves.

When his mother was training their dog Nala not to jump up on people, she would tell Atticus over and over again, "Just ignore her when she does that. Even if you yell at her, she likes the attention, whether it's negative or positive. So just ignore her. When she does something good, praise her. She'll start behaving to get the positive attention."

If they could teach Nala—who was not the brightest dog in the pound—not to jump, surely they could teach people not to hate (or be so stupid). Nala, as it turned out, was a pretty smart dog. She just needed to be taught some manners. When she sat down and showed Atticus her paw, she was praised. When she jumped—something she didn't even do anymore—she was ignored.

When people are stupid, they shouldn't be allowed to get attention. It was the same with the kids at school doing bad things. It was the same with the person who wrote what he or she wrote to Molly. So even as Mr. Gulf tried to handle it all very discreetly, word got out quickly. By the end of the day, Kevin Thurston was called into the office and questioned.

Most of the kids hung around the school after the final bell to see what was going to happen. Several kids had been called into Mr. Gulf's office—Kyle Patrick, Connor Pearson, Cameron Norris, Jeff Borden, Jeremy Thomas, and Kevin Thurston. One by one, the players came out. Only Kevin remained.

As Trevor and Atticus rolled past people, they could hear them talking about Molly Vickers and what had happened. While no one was exactly sure, the rumors were flying. Whatever it was, Molly had been crying. There was, of course, immediate speculation that this had to be the work of Kevin Thurston and his apelike friends. They were, after all, the only people to be called into the office. And they had been the only ones to really protest Molly's position on the team. Still, when Kevin finally did emerge from the office, no one said a thing. Everyone began to pile out of the school as if it were just any other day. What kid in his or her right mind would ask Kevin if the rumors were true?

What kid except Trevor Smith, the rebel with a cause. The rebel with a cause who kept forgetting his best friend couldn't run away like he could.

"Hey, that was real intelligent," Trevor said in the general, but not specific, direction of Kevin Thurston. Kevin was, Atticus noted, standing in the center of about 15 other football players.

They had all been standing in the main parking lot of the school when Trevor called out. Everyone stopped.

82

"This is not good strategy," Atticus said over his shoulder to Trevor. They had played warship games on Trevor's computer many times, and Trevor had proven himself to be a good strategist. This was not one of those times.

Trevor ignored him and stared back at the open, gaping-mouthed jocks who couldn't believe Trevor Smith and his geeky little sidekick had the audacity to speak out loud to them. In public.

"Are you talking to me?" Kevin asked disbelievingly.

Trevor continued to stare right at him.

"Are you talking to me?" he asked again. Trevor didn't flinch. Atticus did. He counted the number of football players staring back at them.

This was not good strategy.

A small crowd began to form around them.

"Am I lookin' at anyone else?"

"You think I did this?" Kevin snorted, throwing a hand up against his own chest, feigning innocence.

Atticus squirmed in his seat, looking nervously around at all the kids who were now moving closer to get a better listen to what was going on. Freaks hovered, and geeks chewed nervously on their fingers.

Far off to the edge of the parking lot, Atticus

spotted a gaggle of beauties. And right in the middle was the fair Molly Vickers. Crying. Atticus felt a lump form in his throat. She had her head bent down and was crying while some of the other girls tried to console her. She was probably embarrassed and scared and mad all at the same time. Atticus could feel anger welling up inside him. All she had wanted to do was play football. All she wanted to do was what she did best, which was play sports.

Then, for a brief moment, Molly looked up. She raised her head to brush her bangs from her eyes, and it happened. She locked eyes with Atticus. No doubt, she had looked up to where the ruckus was. She was probably checking to see what the beastly Kevin Thurston was doing. She probably still couldn't believe her one-time friend had turned on her so viciously. Whatever the reasons, she locked eyes with Atticus. At that very moment, Atticus grew three times in size. He was no longer a little tugboat. He was a fully loaded battleship ready for war. Suddenly . . .

"Man, you have the brains of a hamster. And a dumb one at that," came a voice. It was loud. It was powerful. It was Atticus.

Trevor jumped. Mouths fell open to an all-time record chin drop. And Atticus could feel the eyes of all the beauties staring at him while he berated

Kevin Thurston and his stupid little prank in front of the whole school. There was no strategy now. He was flying by the seat of his pants and saying things to Kevin Thurston that he had been meaning to say for years.

This was just the kind of typical bully behavior that only a no-good, spineless, whiny baby would pull. Only someone who wasn't smart enough or brave enough or strong enough resorted to behind-the-back kinds of scare tactics, and, frankly, Atticus was sick of it. He was sick of hearing about it. He was sick of reading about it. He was even sicker to think it was now in his own school.

Intellectually, Atticus knew that the thing to do was ignore Kevin and his behavior completely. But in matters of the heart, intellect wasn't always considered.

"You know how moths are so stupid that they fly right into the lights and burn themselves up? That's you. Man, you're so stupid, it's a wonder you make it to school every day. We should just all be thankful you can remember how to get here. 'Course, that would explain why you're so stupid in class. You used up all your brain cells just getting here."

There was a strange moment of silence. Except, of course, for the gasps uttered by a few geeks sprinkled here and there. Then . . .

"Argh!" In a mad dash, Kevin Thurston broke from his ranks and came charging at Trevor and Atticus. Trevor had just enough time to pull Atticus's chair backward, give it a hard jerk to the left, and begin peeling away from Kevin.

Atticus could feel the power kick into Trevor's legs. Trevor would later call this "sheer terror." Atticus could feel all the beauties looking at him. He could feel Molly Vickers smiling at him for sticking up for her.

He could hear kids yelling. He could hear the pounding of footsteps as nearly half the team charged after him and Trevor. He could hear Trevor breathing heavily, and, mostly, he could hear Trevor asking, "Are you insane?!" as they wheeled away.

It hadn't been good strategy, and the odds were stacked against them. There was an entire fleet of football players, and there were only two of them. They were outnumbered and out-gunned.

Trevor had gone about ten feet before Atticus heard the sounds of Trevor getting hit. Hard. He had been running for the bushes, hoping to break through the bushes and make a break for it through the field. They had two choices—make a break for the bushes and open field or run to the teachers for help. Both Atticus and Trevor would rather face Kevin and his gang than have the entire school see them run for the teachers. Trevor had almost reached the end of the pavement when Atticus felt the chair pull back sharply. He knew instantly that Trevor had been caught. He had been jerked backward, pulling the chair with him before he could let go. Then, in the next moment, he was flying past Atticus. He curled up into a ball as soon as he hit and rolled a bit. At least three boys were on top of him in an instant. Atticus and his chair were left suddenly alone, spinning in a circle while the mob rushed past him, piling onto Trevor.

Atticus managed to get his hands on top of the wheels to steady his chair. He readjusted himself and moved forward, hollering at Kevin and his buddies to leave Trevor alone, but it was no use. No one could hear a thing. There was a sudden rush of kids. Everyone ran forward to see the fight, with some idiot—as there is always apt to be one—yelling, "Fight! Fight!"

Trevor was lost in the sea of bodies. Atticus tried frantically to move around people to see his friend, but kids were rushing past him, jarring his chair out of the way. He could hear the sounds of a fight and the comments being made by onlookers.

Oooh!
Oh, man!
That's gotta hurt!
Get 'em, Trevor!
Hey, he's on his feet!
"Run!" someone screamed helpfully.

Atticus couldn't take it any longer. It was his fault they were piling on top of Trevor. It was his big mouth. Trevor needed him. Without another thought, he began madly ramming his chair through the crowds, forcing people to back up.

"Move! Move! Move!" he hollered until, at last, he was up front where he should be. He could see the pile again. Only, it was not a pile anymore. Connor Pearson, Kyle Patrick, Jeff Borden, and some of the others had formed a semicircle around Cameron Norris as he held Trevor's arms behind his back. Without a word exchanged between them, the boys instinctively knew to form this semicircle so that the teachers couldn't see right away who was doing what to whom. It was some sort of ritualistic thing that these players had learned at the local Bullies-R-Us seminar, and Atticus was determined to break through it.

Kevin Thurston was moving forward as though he were going to start punching Trevor in the stomach, while Cameron held Trevor up.

Trevor was struggling fiercely. He was kicking out his legs at Kevin, causing Kevin to move around him, trying to get in on Trevor from the side.

Atticus took a deep breath. His heart began beating wildly. Blood was surging through his body, and with one final deep breath, Atticus shoved his hands down on the tops of the wheels. Grasping them firmly with both hands, Atticus shoved down hard and lurched the chair forward.

Again, Atticus shoved down hard. It took only three hard pushes before he had picked up good speed. And, as though every kid knew what was about to happen, they stepped to the side, parting like the Red Sea (of Walnut Middle School). Atticus didn't close his eyes. He didn't bring up his hands to shield his face and body from the impact. He just plowed straight into the back of Kevin Thurston, hitting him hard and causing him to fall over to the right of the chair. There was a gigantic "Oooh!" from the crowd, which promptly fell silent. So quiet, in fact, that every kid at Walnut Middle School heard how hard Kevin Thurston hit the ground. It would be a hit and a fall that kids would talk about for months to come. It would be known as "the pavement hit" or "the blindsided-chair hit." It was beautiful. It was pure poetry. If ever there was a time Atticus was glad to have his chair, if ever there was a time he was happy with how heavy and cumbersome the chair could be, this was it. This was truly Atticus Weaver's finest moment.

With traffic not 200 feet away, an airplane flying overhead, birds chirping in nearby trees, and the *ooh*-ing and *ahh*-ing of several hundred kids, never had the parking lot seemed so disbelievingly quiet. All eyes were on Kevin as he rolled off to one side, shook his head, and fixed his gaze upon his assailant.

"You!" he hissed, slowly getting to his feet.

Everything was perfectly still.

Atticus could hear his own breathing now, which was short and labored. It was difficult to suck in a sufficient amount of air, and he thought, just for a moment, that he might pass out.

Focus. Focus. Don't show your fear. Look him in the eye. Don't let him see you sweat.

He was sweating.

Profusely.

No one spoke while Kevin Thurston stood fully. He brushed himself off for a moment.

The Fight

Birds chirping, the faint sound of traffic, teachers moving in for the rescue—they were all small, distant sounds unmatched by the pounding of his own heart.

Kevin looked up from his clothes and squinted at Atticus.

"You little punk," he said.

Suddenly, breaking the eerie silence of the parking lot, Trevor went wild. He began thrashing around, kicking and squirming out of Cameron's grasp. Kyle Patrick had to step in to help hold Trevor back.

"Don't touch him!" Trevor demanded. "You leave him alone!"

"Shut up!" Kevin said over his shoulder and moved closer to Atticus.

Atticus's heart absolutely could not take this. It was the moment he had thought he was waiting for. This was it. This was his black eye. *What?* What had he been thinking? Was he insane? He licked his lips and gripped his wheels. He thought about lurching forward again, ramming Kevin's legs. He thought about pulling a 180. He had gotten good at that.

He could have avoided Kevin long enough for the teachers to come in. He could hear them now. They were coming. Help was coming.

"Don't touch him!" Trevor's voice was almost frantic.

But Atticus Weaver stood firm. He braced himself. He braced the wheels. He was ready to take whatever this creep could dish out. For honor. For dignity. For Molly Vickers!

This was it! This was it!

"Naw! I'm not going to waste my time on a cripple," Kevin Thurston said.

Atticus blinked.

The words pounded down on Atticus. To have been hit by a falling piano would have been about the same. It took Atticus's breath away momentarily, and all he could do was blink.

There was some laughing from some of Kevin's friends. There was the release of Trevor and the sudden emergence of Mr. Gulf through the crowd. None of it mattered. Nothing mattered. Atticus could only sit in stunned silence. He couldn't move. Not his hands. Not his mouth. Even his eyes were transfixed on Kevin Thurston.

Just as he was released from their grip, Trevor was given a final push in the middle of his shoulders by Kyle Patrick, causing him to stumble forward. There were a few grumbles from the crowd about this. Or maybe it was still about what Kevin had said. Atticus didn't know.

It didn't matter. In front of the entire school, with everyone watching, with every representative from every clique, Kevin Thurston had delivered the most debilitating, painful, vicious blow Atticus Weaver had ever received.

Oh, sure. He had heard it all before. He had heard little kids ask their mothers about his chair when they were out in public. He had heard other kids whisper (loudly) about his chair, wondering what was wrong with him. No one ever asked him directly but always guessed as though there were some grand prize to be awarded to the winner. There had even been jokes made by some kids over the years. They were infrequent, but they had been there. Atticus was used to that. He was prepared for those kinds of remarks, made from either ignorance or meanness. But this.

Atticus Weaver had been prepared to be a martyr. He had readied himself for the black eye that would stand as a symbol. He had been ready to take on Kevin Thurston and his kind. Instead of being some kind of hero, as he had dreamed, he had been embarrassed and humiliated in front of everyone. Kevin Thurston had reacted in a most unexpected way. Atticus Weaver was so insignificant that even the biggest, meanest bully in the school couldn't be bothered by him.

Mr. Gulf was there, telling everyone to move away. Someone was yelling that all the kids should be getting on home, that they needed to be on their way. Someone was asking Atticus if he was okay.

No. No, he wasn't.

At one moment his heart had been pounding so hard it felt as if it could pound right out of his chest. He had felt more frightened and alive and excited than he had ever been. He had faced and readied himself for the biggest, most monumental event of his life and within the same moment was completely shut down.

This was supposed to be the moment that he was going to show Molly Vickers what he was made of. This was supposed to be the moment that he was going to show the entire school. This was supposed to be the moment when Atticus Weaver single-handedly took Kevin Thurston down.

He thought for a moment that his heart had stopped. As suddenly as that.

One moment it was pounding so hard. The next, he wasn't sure it was even working anymore.

No, he wasn't all right.

Everyone had seen. Molly Vickers had seen. He didn't even rate a hit. He didn't matter at all.

The Fight

Cripple. He had called Atticus a cripple.

No one had laughed hard. It hadn't been a joke. So everyone thought Atticus was a cripple, too, and just went along with what Kevin said. Was that it? Was this what everyone thought, and only Kevin, in a moment of anger, was able to say it?

"Are you okay?" Trevor asked as he got next to Atticus.

Atticus didn't look up. He still looked after Kevin as Kevin and his friends walked away. Mr. Gulf was hot on their trail, calling after them.

It was difficult to hear what was being said, but Mr. Gulf was talking to all the boys, shaking his finger. Kevin Thurston was shrugging his shoulders, feigning innocence as he always did. And he always got away with everything. It didn't matter what he did. He would always get away with things because someone would always bail him out. Coach Powell mostly. The coach wanted his star player out of trouble. He wanted Kevin to be able to play ball. Without Kevin Thurston, it would be difficult to win any games.

Slowly, the crowds broke away. One by one, kids headed out of the parking lot. As soon as they got home, they would forget all about this afternoon. Not Atticus.

He hated Kevin.

He had never really liked Kevin, it was true. But, he hadn't actually *hated*. He hadn't hated anyone before. It was, as his mother pointed out, a lot of wasted energy. But, now, watching Kevin as he threw sideways grins and winks to his friends, Atticus Weaver hated him like no person had hated another person before.

This was the worst day of his life.

"Hey, you okay?" Trevor leaned forward, trying to get his friend's attention. "I said, 'Are you okay?' They didn't hurt you, did they?"

Atticus finally looked back at Trevor and watched his friend for a minute. Trevor's shirt was torn, his hair was all messed up, and there were dirt smudge marks on his face, neck, and arms.

No, he wasn't all right.

"Yeah," Atticus said with the heaviest heart possible. "I'm fine."

THE FALLOUT

WHATEVER happened on Monday was nothing compared to what the next day would bring. And, to his great disappointment, Atticus had missed it all. He had not gone to school the following day. He told his mother he was sick, saying that he thought he might have overexerted himself. Saying that was the one sure way to stay home. Mrs. Weaver was always worried about Atticus "overexerting" himself.

In truth, Atticus couldn't bear to face anyone at school. If it was possible, he hoped never to see anyone again. He had seen the looks on their faces. He had seen how everyone avoided eye contact with him after Kevin had called him what he called him. The word still rang in his ears. He still felt the hurt in his heart.

Atticus tried to push the events of the previous day from his mind, and Mrs. Weaver gave him the perfect distraction.

"Look at this," she said, tossing a newspaper at him. Atticus was still in his bed, waiting to see if she would go to work. He had hoped, faintly, that he could spend the day alone. Deep down, however, he knew that would never happen. Mrs. Weaver lived in fear that he would somehow fall out of his chair and not be able to help himself. Atticus had shown his mother a dozen times how he could get in and out of his chair. It wasn't always easy, it was true. But he could do it. How did she think he bathed himself? But she lived to worry about him.

"What is it?" he asked without looking at it.

"It's from the local paper. The reporter who did that article on Molly Vickers." She pointed to the paper so he would read the rest.

Atticus found a small picture of the reporter smiling back at him. Next to it was the question in large caption: SHOULD GIRLS PLAY FOOTBALL? WHAT DO YOU THINK? It was an invitation for people to log on to the reporter's Web site and offer their opinions.

"She's your friend, isn't she? You ought to get online and stick up for her," Mrs. Weaver said, leaning against the doorway.

"Are you going to go to work today?" Atticus asked her, ignoring the paper for a moment. She looked surprised and then a little hurt.

"No, I thought I would take the day off. I've

got lots of personal time," she lied. "And I have tons of things I need to get done."

"Mom, you're staying home because of me, and you don't have to," Atticus sighed, letting the paper fall to his side. "I told you, I can take care of myself."

"I know you can. I'm taking a personal day because I have tons of things I have to get done, and I never get to be around you that much. Is that so bad?"

Atticus opened his mouth and then shut it again. For a brief moment, he thought about telling her what had happened the day before. He thought about telling her how he was called a cripple and that it was more important to him than ever that he be trusted to be alone and take care of himself. But he didn't. He just looked at his mother, who stood smiling at him from the doorway.

She had her hair pulled back in a ponytail. Normally, she would have her hair done for work, complete with curls and so much hairspray that Atticus always gagged a little. He told her over and over again she shouldn't do that. He worried that her head was highly flammable. But today, with her ponytail and freshly scrubbed face, she looked like a kid. Like a friend. Telling her to get lost just didn't seem like the right thing to do.

But she was completely clueless about some things.

This was the same woman who had named her child Atticus. This was the same woman who walked around the house singing 40- and 50-year-old songs. She sang songs that were older than she was. She still set out presents from the Easter Bunny and Santa Claus. Atticus wondered why his mother didn't see that a large bunny hopping from house to house all over the country, hiding eggs and giving presents, was highly improbable. Or that a really fat guy flying around in a sled loaded down by presents pulled by eight tiny reindeer was not only unlikely but highly dangerous. And, didn't she ever worry that Atticus would make the connection that the Easter Bunny and Santa Claus had the same handwriting? They just never discussed these things because she liked the idea that he might still believe, and he liked the idea that she liked that.

No, she was better off not knowing about Kevin Thurston and what he had said. Atticus shrugged his shoulders and pulled himself up.

"I promise. You won't even know I'm here," Atticus's mom said, disappearing from his room. And with the exception of bringing him breakfast and, later, lunch, she was true to her word. Although, she could have thrown a wild party and he would never have known. He became so engrossed in the computer that he lost all track of time. It had been easy for him to completely forget about Kevin Thurston and get lost in the World Wide Web and all the wonderful bits of information it had to offer. Atticus played around on the Internet for hours.

It was not until he stretched, allowing his eyes to wander around his room, that he saw the newspaper again and remembered to write in his opinion about the girl football player.

The reporter had posted comments sent in about his article and the idea of a girl football player. As Atticus read through the letters, he found most were quite positive. He skimmed most of those. It was the letters that protested Molly Vickers making the team that really caught his attention.

Many were from parents saying they didn't like the idea of their sons playing against a girl. The common complaint was that they were afraid that either the girl would get hurt or, because their sons were trying hard not to hurt the girl, that it would bring the game down.

Atticus skimmed these as well. It was not until he got to the letter from a football player from another school that he really paid attention. A kid who asked to be anonymous said that if he had to play against Molly, he would purposefully hit her hard. He said that if she really wanted to know what football was all about, then she deserved to feel what a full-body hit felt like too. There were a few more letters from other boys promising much of the same treatment.

Atticus studied the letters. All but three were anonymous. The other three had their user names posted. MSpiezio and danservo1 hinted that they were players from another school within the same city district. Ticktock wasn't as subtle.

"Without their star player (Kevin Thurston) and playing a girl for kicker, Walnut is finished for the season. I don't know why anyone would even bother giving them space in the sports section." It went on to say other things, mostly repeats of what the others had said. There was the promise of hitting Molly Vickers and hitting her as hard, if not harder, than the boys on the field.

There were plenty of things Atticus would have liked to say in response to the letters. Instead, he went back through the Web looking for sites that talked about disabilities.

He found chat rooms and scores of information. What was he looking for? A sudden cure? Some grand announcement he might have missed? He reread information that he knew so well, he was sure it was actually branded somewhere in the back of his brain.

Discouraged or tired or both, he turned off the computer and went out to the living room to watch some television. He found his mother sitting on the couch, curled up and watching an old movie. She was wearing sweatpants, an oversized T-shirt, and fuzzy slippers. She jumped a little and looked embarrassed when she saw him.

"I know I need to be doing other things," she said, grinning. "But I found this old movie."

By freak standards, Atticus wasn't supposed to like his mother. He wasn't sure about the jock, beauty, cheerleader, or geek standards. The beauty of being an outcast was there were no set standards as to how he was supposed to behave, and so it was easy for him to go on liking his mother. She was a great mom. He wasn't embarrassed to admit that to anyone. She had done so much for him. She had been there for him after his father left them. She loved him so much. So what if she named him Atticus? She liked to tell him it was from the book *To Kill a*

Mockingbird, but he sometimes wondered if it wasn't because of the movie that starred an old actor named Gregory Peck. She was forever going on about what a stud he was. The guy looked like he was nearly 100 in the movie that was made 40 years ago, but she loved it, and she loved the actor. It was just another thing about his mother that made him laugh to himself.

She loved ice cream and chocolate. She loved to fly kites and tell scary stories. She snorted when she laughed, which always embarrassed her and made her laugh even harder. And she loved old movies.

"It's a William Powell/Myrna Loy picture, *The Thin Man*," she said excitedly, as though any of this would mean anything to Atticus. He stared blankly at her. "Oh, never mind. Come here." She patted the side of the couch for him to come closer to her.

And together, for the rest of the afternoon, they watched the movie that seemed incredibly silly and boring to Atticus. The Thin Man, as he was called, was really this detective. Only he kept telling everyone he wasn't a detective anymore. He said he had retired, but no one believed him. Instead, his wife really wanted to be one and kept trying to solve this crime, only the skinny guy was afraid she would get hurt, so he ran around after her trying to keep her out of trouble. By the end, he had solved the mystery of who did what. But really, the only reason he got the mystery solved was because he was following his wife around.

It was difficult to keep from yawning.

Frankly, they all looked alike. All the women had bleached blonde hair, all the men had black hair, and everyone overacted. Only the wife was different. She had dark hair. And if there was any character he could identify with, it would be the one whom no one else believed in. He knew what *that* felt like. He wrinkled his nose, wishing he were watching something else. Anything else.

The phone rang, and Atticus popped a wheelie trying to get to it.

Saved by the bell.

It was Trevor. Atticus looked at the clock. Time had flown by.

"You're not even going to believe what happened in school today!" Trevor started in right away.

"What?"

"Well, you remember what happened yesterday?" he started.

Like Atticus was going to forget. He rolled his eyes to himself and leaned back in his chair.

"Yeah," he said slowly.

"Well, get this. Someone left an anonymous

not in the office that said that they saw Kevin Thurston putting the note on Molly's locker."

"That's no surprise," Atticus said. "Everyone knows he did it. He's the one who's been protesting her being on the team the whole time."

Atticus caught Mrs. Weaver turning her head slightly toward him, so he lowered his voice.

"He was the one who told the guys to rush her in the tryouts, remember? Everyone knows that he didn't want her to make the team."

"Well, I guess they proved it was him, and guess what? He got suspended from school today and kicked off the football team. How about that?"

Atticus sat forward in his chair.

Suspended!

"Suspended?"

Mrs. Weaver looked over at Atticus. "Who?" she mouthed at him.

There was no way to tell her everything that was going on without getting into the whole story. It just wasn't something Atticus wanted to do.

"Just some stupid kid," he whispered, waving his hand at her. She mouthed, "Oh," and returned to her movie. She had to pay particularly close attention to the characters as everyone looked exactly alike.

"Hey, instant message me," Atticus told Trevor and hung up. Without another word to his mother, Atticus went back to his room and got online.

Trevor was there in a matter of minutes.

Aticus8: So, I bet everyone is going crazy. I can't believe he got suspended.

TSJr4: I heard Coach Powell was in Mr. Gulf's office all afternoon yelling about it. He wants to know who left the note.

Aticus8: Someone left a note?

TSJr4: Yeah, that's what I heard. Someone left a note telling Mr. Gulf that they had seen Kevin putting the note on Molly's locker.

Aticus8: Yeah, but he couldn't suspend Kevin with only the proof of a note.

TSJr4: That's what I heard. Anyway, he did. And Kevin is telling everyone he didn't do it.

Aticus8: Yeah, sure he didn't.

TSJr4: He swears it up and down. He was crying when he left the school.

Aticus8: He was crying?

There was a part of Atticus who was glad to hear this and had wished deeply that he had been there to see it. What had Kevin expected? There had to be fallout from what he had done. He had upset too many people. He had been mean for too long to too many people. Finally, he had gone too far, and now he was paying for it. People were sick of this kind of stupid behavior. It was such a wimpy thing to do. Now he would pay and pay dearly. The one thing that Kevin Thurston cared about more than anything else was football. He lived and breathed football.

TSJr4: Crying like a baby. His dad came and picked him up. Amy Loe says she was standing outside when he was crying to his dad, swearing that he didn't do anything to Molly.

Aticus8: Too bad for Coach Powell

TSJr4: Yeah, he's super mad. Everyone is.

Aticus8: At Kevin?

TSJr4: Yeah, because he was being so stupid. Now the whole team is going to stink without him. And Amy Loe is going on and on because our first game is against Blendon.

Aticus8: They're always good.

TSJr4: They're going to clean our clocks. Are you going to go? I was going to go if you want.

Had Trevor asked Atticus to go that morning, Atticus would have said, "No way." There was no way he wanted to lay his eyes on Kevin Thurston. But things had changed. Now that Kevin was no longer on the football team, Atticus was interested. He really did want to see Molly Vickers in her debut game.

Aticus8: Yeah. I'll go if you want.

Occasionally, there would come a time when both boys would sit staring at their monitors, neither one typing anything. This was one of those times. They had said about as much as one could say on this topic and were being careful about what else to say. Being such good friends, they each knew what the other was thinking about and didn't want to say. The real issue, the real fallout of the "blindsided-chair hit" and everything that came after was one of those unpleasant things that no one really likes to talk about but needs to before things can move forward.

Finally, Atticus began to type something about his day on the Web when Trevor's message came up.

TSJr4: So, are you going to come back to school tomorrow? Now that Kevin is gone, you don't need to worry about that.

Aticus8: I'm not worried about Kevin.

TSJr4: I know. I just wanted to let you know that he was gone.

Aticus8: Yeah, I'll be back.

Several more minutes ticked off the clock as both boys sat staring at their computers. Finally . . .

TSJr4: Okay, I'll see ya tomorrow. Gotta go.

Atticus signed off.

So, Kevin Thurston was suspended from school and kicked off the football team. Couldn't have happened to a nicer guy.

THE GAME

WITH Kevin Thurston out of school for the remainder of the week, going back to school was easy enough for Atticus. No one talked to him about the incident in the parking lot. No one cared. All anyone could talk about was the big game. Before he knew it, Atticus was back in the groove of doing homework and hanging out with Trevor. But Friday brought renewed tensions. People were arguing in the hallways again. They were talking about how they thought Molly Vickers would do in her first game.

Amy Loe had heard that some of the players from Blendon said they were going to cream Molly. Amy knew a girl who was friends with some of the cheerleaders over at Blendon, and she said they were talking about it all the time. They were all saying that with Kevin gone, there would be no passing game, which meant the Walnut players would have to run. Blendon was ready for that. And they were saying that once they got a good hit on Molly Vickers, she would

111

be so afraid to go back out there, she would start missing the kicks. With Kevin Thurston off the team and Molly Vickers kicking, Blendon was very confident about winning.

Bad news travels fast, Atticus guessed. But with a girl like Amy Loe around, it was no wonder everyone knew about every little thing that happened at school.

The other rumor, according to Amy Loe, was that Kevin Thurston was going to come to the football game. It was a rumor that turned out to be true.

Atticus and Trevor, as always, were able to be down in front of the bleachers, not 20 feet from the field and 10 feet from the cheerleaders. They had been busily watching the girls cheer when they saw some of the girls suddenly start whispering among themselves and looking over toward the stairs of the bleachers. Atticus looked over his shoulder, following the gaze of Amy Loe and company. Sure enough, Kevin Thurston appeared. With his hands shoved deep into his pockets, he avoided all eye contact. He was with about eight other jocks. All out-of-seasoners, but they made for good company in his time of need.

Predictably, they all headed up toward the top row of the bleachers. But this journey was particularly difficult for Kevin. It was football. He didn't want to be going farther away. He wanted to be going closer. Still, with head down, he followed quietly behind his jock friends.

As he passed each row, geeks, freaks, and beauties (and their respective parents) watched carefully.

There goes Kevin Thurston.

That's the one. He's the one who wrote the note.

Him? Really?

Why would he do that? He was a really good football player.

That was really stupid. Now he can't play at all.

That's him.

He's the one I was telling you about.

There's Kevin Thurston.

At the sound of the whistle, however, all eyes were back on the field, and Kevin Thurston was momentarily forgotten about.

The game had begun. And really, the outcome depended on how you looked at it. If you believed that Walnut was going to get crushed because they didn't have Kevin Thurston playing, then it was a success. But if you had hoped that Walnut might somehow still win the game because for the last ten years in a row Walnut had beaten Blendon, then it might have been considered a disappointing game.

Kevin Thurston wasn't just any player. He played quarterback on offense and cornerback on defense. He was on the field at all times. Acting as team captain, he had been the chief motivating force. His absence from the field left a huge hole. While Kyle Patrick was well liked by his teammates, he didn't have the same personality on the field as his friend. And he just didn't have the kind of arm Kevin had.

Kyle Patrick tried very hard to throw the ball to his receivers, Jeff Borden and Carlos Munoz. Almost every time the ball was thrown and caught, the receivers were stopped immediately, making the game very long. The Walnut Cougars tried again and again to drive the ball down the field but just couldn't do it. Blendon was big this year. And they were very motivated. After each play, the Blendon players would leap wildly into the air, high-fiving one another and smacking one another very hard on the helmets. An activity, Atticus was sure, that led to many of the "dumb jock" jokes.

Several times, Kyle tried to hand the ball off to Cameron Norris to let him run it down the field. As strong as Cameron was, he just couldn't take it all the way down. Two, three, four guys

from Blendon would pile up on Cameron, and
he would be down within a couple of yards. And
several times, Kyle fumbled the ball. Groans
filled the air each time. Since they were in
elementary school together playing in the youth
leagues, Kyle had always played second-string to
Kevin. Now was his time to shine, but he was
doing miserably. He had grown comfortable
watching his friend do it all. Now, suddenly, the
spotlight was on him to lead his team to victory.

All the screaming everyone was doing didn't
seem to help. Even poor Amy Loe was going
hoarse, she was screaming so loud. But the
Blendon team had effectively shut down the
Cougars.

In the second quarter, the Cougars were
able to score a touchdown. Carlos Munoz caught
a beautiful pass and managed to slip past the
Blendon players. He barely made his way into
the end zone. Everyone went crazy. For one
thing, it would be the first time everyone would
see Molly Vickers.

As she stepped out onto the field, the fans
went nuts. People were yelling and screaming,
and Amy Loe reached a whole new level of noise
making. But Molly looked as if she couldn't hear
them at all. She was still listening to the coach
even as she started to run out onto the field.

With her helmet already on, she was trotting backward, nodding her head furiously at whatever the coach was yelling at her.

Atticus licked his lips. Molly was new to the team. There hadn't been a lot of time for her to practice with them. He wondered if the Walnut players would protect her this time. Would they open up the hole and let the Blendon players come crashing through, or could they hold them? *Would* they hold them? With Connor Pearson on the line, Atticus had to be hopeful. Suddenly, Atticus could feel knots forming in his stomach.

"Come on, Molly," he said under his breath.

The crowd was screaming.

The coach was pacing back and forth, half afraid to watch, half afraid of missing anything.

Atticus could see Jeremy Thomas talking to Molly out on the field. Again, she was nodding. Even from where she stood, Atticus could tell she was nervous. He had watched her long enough as a beauty and a cheerleader to know her, to know her body language. She was scared. But she was focused.

"Come on, Molly," Atticus heard Trevor mutter beside him.

The snap was good.

The ball was hiked perfectly to Jeremy, who

caught it and set it up for Molly. Time seemed to move so slowly.

"Come on, Molly," someone else said.

Connor Pearson was standing upright. He was battling against another player who seemed to be twice Connor's size. Every Walnut player seemed to be tied up with a Blendon player. Then it seemed like the Walnut line started to cave, and the blue jerseys of Blendon came crashing through.

Molly had moved forward. Nervous though she was, she waited until the ball was in position just the way she and Jeremy had practiced. She took three running strides forward and blasted the ball with her right foot. At the precise moment that the wall caved and the blue jerseys came storming in, the ball was up and flying out of anyone's reach. It went higher and higher. It sailed right through the uprights. Goal!

Smack!

Molly hadn't even had enough time to see her own kick followed through before she was hit at full impact. One of the Blendon players tore past Derek Huling and Connor Pearson and hit Molly on the right side. She collapsed like a rag doll. The crowd was on its feet, cheering for the goal before they realized she was hit and down.

Connor Pearson broke from the line. He turned and charged the Blendon player who had hit Molly. When he was about two feet from the guy, Connor pushed off the ground, making a flying tackle-leap, and the two players rolled over each other and hit the ground hard. A whistle was blown. More players piled on. It was a full-fledged fight. Another whistle was blown, and Coach Powell was on the field, arms waving wildly.

Boos infiltrated the bleachers. Hisses and yells demanded that the referee do something about that unsportsmanlike hit. But the poor referee couldn't hear a thing. He was far too busy trying to pull boys off one another. Atticus couldn't see Molly anywhere on the field.

It was frustrating to sit in his chair, jerking his body from left to right and craning his neck to see anything. It was impossible to see past the rush of people now on the field. Finally, with a final whistle blow and every head and assistant coach on the field, the fights were disbanded. Atticus could see Molly. She was all right. With the field quiet once again, the referee was able to do his job. He put his arms up, indicating the kick was good. And there would be a penalty on Blendon. More cheers came from the bleachers as Molly and Jeremy ran off the field together.

Blendon would score three more times before the half was over, leaving the score 20 to 7. Unlike Molly, the kicker for the Blendon team had missed an extra point. Still, the Walnut fans were unhappy to see they were trailing on the scoreboard.

This wouldn't be happening if Kevin were playing, some people grumbled.

If he hadn't been so stupid.

I don't know why he raised such a fuss about that girl playing. She's good.

Yeah, maybe she ought to take over Kevin's old position. Maybe we would be winning then.

He shouldn't have done that.

We could be winning if he was in.

Actually, the outcome of the game didn't mean that much to Atticus or Trevor. Of course, they would have liked for their school to win, but the most interesting part of the game occurred at halftime.

With only two minutes left before the first half was over and Blendon in possession of the ball, Trevor and Atticus decided to go to the concession stand and get a drink and some candy.

"So, what do you think about Molly?" Trevor asked on their way back. Atticus balanced their two jumbo-sized drinks and candy in a drink carrier on his lap while Trevor pushed them along.

"She's awesome," Atticus said a little more enthusiastically than he wished he had. He coughed a little. "She's pretty good. She doesn't seem to get too nervous."

"Boy, she took a pretty good hit."

"Did you see Connor Pearson sticking up for her? That was pretty cool."

"He wants to win." Trevor was always the voice of logic. Except for the fact that it was he who had suggested two super-jumbo drinks, two boxes of Junior Mints, a bag of popcorn, and two corn dogs.

As they headed back to the spot in front of the bleachers and the cheerleaders, the halftime whistle was blown, and players began to rush past them, making their way to the locker rooms. At the mouth of the gate that surrounded the field, Trevor pulled Atticus out of the way as they waited to let the crowd pass.

The Walnut team passed first, and Atticus could hear various Cougars talking about the score. They were mad. They wanted to win. There were complaints that the Blendon team was cheating. It was typical jock talk, Atticus supposed. And for a fleeting moment, he saw Molly as she jogged by. People from the stands cheered her name.

Then a much more animated, vocal crowd moved through the gates—Blendon.

"Oh, yeah!"

"I told you, man! I told you we would win!" One player was slapping his friend and fellow teammate on the back.

"With Thurston gone, this thing is wrapped up!"

"Oh, yeah!"

"Tick tock! Tick tock!"

"We're going to win."

Atticus watched the big number 76 as his jersey blended in with the rest of the players and disappeared from sight.

Tick tock.

It was an odd thing to say. Perhaps, Atticus pondered, it was some sort of nickname.

"Bunch of jerks," Trevor muttered under his breath, pushing Atticus forward again when the crowd cleared.

What was that he said?

With a bump, Atticus was startled back into present thought. As Trevor pushed the chair back onto the surrounding track, the wheels bumped on the uneven surface, spilling a little bit of their sodas on his lap.

Trevor didn't even notice. He was too busy

staring at the cheerleaders from the other team. As was custom, they ran over at halftime, leading a cheer for the other school. The Walnut cheerleaders politely sat back and watched as the Blendon cheerleaders did their bit, and everyone cheered.

Only then did Trevor lean down to take one of the drinks and grinned at Atticus.

"No bloomers yet."

So far, it had been a bloomer-free night.

"What was that he said?" Atticus wondered out loud.

"No bloomers," Trevor said again, watching as Amy Loe now led the cheer for Walnut. It was funny. She was the only cheerleader who didn't use a megaphone. She didn't need one. There was the distinct possibility that if she did use one, she might blow a few people off the highest row of the bleachers. Maybe it was due to safety issues that she didn't own a megaphone.

The Blendon cheerleaders clapped when the Walnut girls were done. Then they all started talking to one another. Amy appeared to know quite a few of the other girls and was chatting it up happily.

With the sideshow over, more students and parents came down from the bleachers to go to the concession stand. Kevin Thurston was no

exception. But if he thought he could slip through
the crowd unnoticed, he was wrong.

"Hey, Kevin! Nice work," someone yelled,
and Kevin whipped his head over to see who it
was. It came from the general freak direction, but
there was no way to be sure. It was easy for all the
kids to be braver under the cover of night and
about three dozen or so parents sprinkled
throughout the stands.

"Way to be there for your team, Thurston,"
came another voice.

Atticus scanned the stands to see who was
yelling, but no one stood out. There was a
suspicious gaggle of geeks snickering in the
middle of the stands, but it was hard to know if
they had yelled it or were just responding to the
heckler.

Sporting events were different from pep
rallies. At the football game, the geeks liked to
hang in the middle so they could blend into the
crowd. The freaks liked to hang down toward the
front of the bleachers so they could slip under the
bleachers and cause trouble or do whatever it was
that they liked to do down there.

Still again, there were more whispers.

That's Kevin Thurston.

Oh, that's Kevin Thurston.

*Say, isn't he the boy who got himself kicked off
the team?*

Yeah, that's him.

We sure could use him right now.

Atticus watched as Kevin turned back and made his way down the rest of the bleachers, his head hanging low. It was hard to believe, but there was actually a part of Atticus that felt bad for Kevin Thurston. Kevin was miserable.

Atticus munched on his corn dog and turned his attention back to the Walnut marching band. Speaking of miserable . . .

"Man, they stink," Trevor said, reading his friend's thoughts. Yet, this was not clear to the group of geeks who sat transfixed while their buddies performed.

Atticus managed to get the last of his corn dog down and chased it with several sips of his soda. *What was it that kid said?*

"What's with you?" Trevor asked, leaning in toward Atticus and taking a box of Junior Mints from his lap.

"Huh? Oh, just something that I heard. I can't . . ." he began muttering more to himself. It was something that bothered him and would continue to do so for the rest of the game.

The game did not improve much either. While Blendon would score only one more touchdown, much of the game was spent down close to Walnut's red zone. Walnut seemed to be frozen in time. There was nothing they could do. Kyle Patrick had been sacked about ten times, and Connor Pearson was getting tired and letting the offensive line break through more and more often. The receivers were virtually shut down. Only Carlos Munoz seemed able to carry the ball, and as small as he was, he was taking a beating. Four and five guys would pile on top of him in a tackle. He was looking tired.

Even Amy Loe grew tired of yelling for a team that just couldn't seem to do anything. That is, until Walnut made a drive with only ten minutes left in the game. Connor Pearson seemed to have renewed strength and was holding off the line with everything he had. Throw after throw, the partnership between Kyle Patrick and Carlos Munoz landed the Walnut Cougars in the Blendon end zone. Touchdown!

The fans went wild with excitement.

Once again, Molly was called out.

Connor snapped the ball. Jeremy caught it, set it down, and readied it for Molly. Just like the last Cougar touchdown, Molly kicked it perfectly through the uprights. And the offensive line charged through, taking a late hit on Molly. Once again, the Blendon team was penalized. Parents and students booed and hissed as the Blendon team trotted off the field, but Atticus couldn't help but think they were true to their word. Just as he had read in the opinion page of the local paper, the players had promised they would hit her and hit her hard to let her know what it was really like to be a football player.

Only this time, Molly stayed on the ground a little longer.

The fans quieted down as the coach and his staff ran out onto the field. Kneeling over her, they helped her to her feet. She shook her head from side to side, and it was clear that she felt a little dizzy.

As Atticus watched Molly being escorted from the field, his own words flooded his head again. *They were true to their words!*

"Trev," Atticus suddenly blurted out.

Trevor looked back at his friend, his mouth stuffed full of candy. He raised his eyebrows at Atticus as it was the only way he could answer.

Before he would say anything more, Atticus turned around in his chair and looked up to the top of the bleachers. There were a few jocks, but not the one Atticus wanted.

"You see Kevin?" he asked Trevor. Trevor immediately looked up toward the top of the bleachers. "No, he's not there. Do you see him somewhere else? Over by the concession stand." There was a good chance that Kevin simply did not want to return to the bleachers after that last barrage of heckling.

"Yeah, I see him," Trevor said. He was standing on his tiptoes, looking through the fence toward the concession stand. Sure enough, Kevin was there with four other out-of-season jocks, drinking sodas and talking. "So what?" He shrugged his shoulders back at Atticus.

"Let's go over there," Atticus said, causing Trevor to nearly choke on his Junior Mint.

"What?!"

"I need to talk to him. Let's go over there."

"Are you nuts? What do you want to talk to that jerk for? Don't you remember the last time we, uh, met?" Trevor guarded his words carefully. Atticus ignored him.

"I gotta ask him something," Atticus started but was interrupted. Suddenly, a loud banging sound erupted from the stands. Both Atticus and Trevor looked up to see every parent, geek, freak, beauty, and jock on his or her feet, stamping and clapping in a rhythmic way that made the boys turn back toward the field.

In the middle of the field was Molly Vickers lining up to try a 40-yard field goal.

The clock was counting down. With only one minute and 40 seconds left, there was no way the Walnut Cougars could win, but that was not what this was about.

The pulsing sound from the bleachers carried over to the field. It almost sounded like a large heart beating. Everyone was waiting to see if she could do it. A 40-yard field goal kick! Forty-six to be exact. The announcer told the crowd that this would be a school record if she made it.

Boom, boom, boom!

Atticus was biting his lip. Trevor was muttering under his breath. The coach and staff were pacing. Carlos Munoz stood on the sidelines with his hands over his head as though he were watching something frightening. And, slowly, Kevin Thurston stepped closer and closer. The sounds of the stamping feet brought him closer to the field, and he watched along with everyone else as the play went into action.

Again, the snap was good. Jeremy caught the ball, placing it down to the field with great precision. No sooner did Connor snap the ball than he began to battle back against the field. Blendon was breaking through the line—fast.

There was no hesitation this time. Molly stepped forward immediately. She could see the line moving in. She could see the two huge guys break past Connor and Jeff Borden. There was no way she couldn't have seen them. But she never flinched. Instead of shrinking back, she moved forward with great determination.

Jeff was down, and the line steamrolled over the top of him. It was an open field. Just as the two Blendon players moved in on Molly, she drilled the ball with a mighty kick. But no sooner did her leg go up past her hip, kicking through the ball, than she received a crushing tackle. For a horrible moment, she was in the air, like the ball, with no one knowing where she was going. Bodies were everywhere. The ball soared overhead, and Molly came crashing down, with the weight of at least one man on top of her.

The stamping and stomping stopped.

There was complete and utter silence for half a second or an eternity. Atticus didn't know which was which. Then the whistle. Score! The goal was made. Molly made school history. But not one player on the field seemed to be aware of it. No one saw the goal. There was a huge pile-on in the middle of the field. Somewhere on the 40- or 35-yard line, there was a mass of bodies.

"Nooo!" came a sudden booming voice beside Atticus and Trevor, causing them both to jump.

Atticus turned to see Kevin Thurston moving forward quickly. He looked concerned. Atticus could tell that he didn't want to see Molly get hurt. He was worried about her.

Atticus studied him for a moment.

Kevin bit his lip anxiously while the officials pulled bodies off the pile.

"You didn't put that letter in her locker, did you?" Atticus suddenly asked. Kevin turned and looked down at Atticus.

"What?" he asked, somewhat distracted. Then, "No, I didn't. I wouldn't do that to her." He looked up and caught Trevor looking at him. Suddenly he became defensive. "Not that anyone believes me, but I didn't." He looked back out to the field.

Cougar fans were stomping their feet again. It didn't matter that Walnut would lose this game. It had been a great game. Molly Vickers had broken the school record for a successful field goal attempt. Happy though Atticus was for Molly, he continued to watch Kevin.

He really was innocent.

Atticus knew that now.

"I believe you," he said quietly, and Kevin looked back at him.

"What?"

"I said, 'I believe you.' You didn't do it. And I might have an idea who did."

★ ★ ★

The
Resolution

★ ★ ★

THE DEFENSE

IN the story *To Kill a Mockingbird*, Atticus Finch defended a man who most everyone believed was guilty of committing a terrible crime. Atticus Finch was appointed to defend him. No one else but Atticus would bother with the man because he was black, and in those days, that was good enough to get you thrown into jail.

But Atticus Finch was a good man and wanted to help. His chief defense, besides the mere fact that he believed Tom when he said he didn't do it, was that Tom couldn't use his left arm. He was accused of a crime that required the use of his left arm. It was similar to someone accusing Atticus Weaver of climbing a tree. Without the use of his legs, it couldn't be done. The jury convicted Tom anyway. They had hated him from the beginning because he was black. Actually, it was a very sad story, and Atticus Weaver decided that there were two best parts in the book. At one point when Atticus Finch started to leave the courthouse, all the black people stood up in honor of him as he passed by. They respected him because he was fair and kind and smart. That was a good part. And also, when Boo Radley came out of nowhere to save the two kids from the *real* bad guy. That was a good scene too.

Atticus Weaver reasoned that all of this was much the same as what was happening to Kevin Thurston. Because he was a football player who hadn't wanted Molly Vickers to play football, it was very easy to believe that he had assaulted her with some kind of threatening letter and mean pictures. He was just like Tom, the likely suspect wrongly accused. But Atticus had seen Kevin's face when he thought Molly was hit too hard on the field. He hadn't cared about the field goal. While everyone else had been watching the ball to see if it was good, Kevin had been watching Molly. That was not the kind of thing a guy would do if he were so mad at someone that he would scare or insult her with nasty letters.

Besides that, now that Atticus thought about it, it was very unlikely that Kevin Thurston would have put a threatening letter in someone's locker. While Kevin wasn't the greatest student in the world, he knew the rules. Kevin Thurston lived and breathed football and would never have done anything that might land him in trouble with the coach. Whoever pulled that stunt hadn't cared about getting thrown off a football team. But they had cared about getting *Kevin* thrown off the team. So much so that they were willing to set him up.

It was with that thought (and several more) that Atticus explained to Kevin that he would have be patient while he figured out a few things.

"So, why do you care?" Kevin had wanted to know.

"Well, did you do it?" Atticus asked.

The game was over, and people streamed past them, but Atticus, Trevor, and Kevin Thurston were in their own world. The three of them stood in a face-off.

"No, I told you I didn't. I told everyone I didn't do it, but," he said, shrugging his shoulders defensively, "who's gonna believe me?"

Atticus nodded. He knew. He understood.

"So, you didn't tell me. Why do you care? We aren't," Kevin said, throwing a sideways glance to Trevor, "friends."

Trevor snorted at this. That was an understatement.

The Defense

But how could Atticus explain this all to a guy like Kevin? Kevin thought about football and being cool. What did Kevin know about honor and dignity? This was all just a stumbling block for Kevin. He would probably go on to be some great athlete. And, as Atticus believed, athletes never learned from their misfortunes. Some terrible crimes had been committed by athletes, and everyone always forgave them because they worshiped what the athletes could do on the field and forgave them for what they did off the field.

But it didn't work that way for Atticus. He had done everything right. He had tried as hard as he could, but he was still an outcast. He would never be the Atticus Finch-type. People would never stand up out of respect for Atticus Weaver. He was more the Boo Radley-type.

Boo Radley was kind of a freaky guy in *To Kill a Mockingbird* whom all the townspeople made fun of. He was mentally disturbed, but no one really knew that. They just knew that he *never* came out of his house. Kids made up stories about him, and everyone became a little afraid of him. In fact, no one even knew what he looked like anymore. But he wasn't a monster, like everyone thought. He was just different, an outcast. And Boo didn't like the idea of being

made some sort of freak, so he went away.
Atticus figured that Boo Radley thought if
people didn't see him anymore, they couldn't
hurt him. The same way Atticus felt when Kevin
called him a cripple in front of the entire school.
Boo was an outcast, much like Trevor and
Atticus were. And now, to some degree, Kevin
was an outcast too.

How could Atticus explain what he was
doing? He shouldn't care about Kevin Thurston.
He shouldn't care at all. In fact, he should be
pointing a finger and laughing at him as a
payback for all the terrible things Kevin had
done to him. But he couldn't. And, well, he
couldn't explain it to himself very well, much
less to Trevor or Kevin.

Atticus opened his mouth to answer in some
way when the sight of Mr. Gulf saved him.

"You stay here," Atticus said to Kevin and
grabbed hold of his wheels, turning in the
direction of Mr. Gulf. Trevor was quick to act,
handing his drink to Atticus and taking control
of the back handles of the chair.

"Where to?" he asked.

"There. Over there," Atticus pointed. Mr.
Gulf was walking across the field, having gone to
shake hands with the winning coach of Blendon.

"Mr. Gulf!" Atticus called out. Mr. Gulf lifted

his chin, looking around the field until his eyes rested on Trevor and Atticus as they approached. He smiled.

"Yes, Atticus. How are you? Trevor."

"Hello, sir," Trevor said in a low voice.

"Mr. Gulf, I was wondering about something," Atticus started.

"Yes?"

"Who told you about Kevin Thurston? I mean, who was it that left a letter in your office? Who said they saw him dropping the note in Molly Vickers locker?"

Mr. Gulf's smile faded quickly, and he drew his eyebrows together.

"I think that is a school affair. You needn't—" he started, but Atticus was quick to cut him off.

"I really need to know. You see, I don't think Kevin did it. I think someone set him up."

Mr. Gulf looked at Atticus curiously. Atticus immediately understood what Mr. Gulf was thinking and agreed.

"I know I would be the last person to think Kevin was innocent. We're not exactly friends. But I don't think he did it."

"Yes, well," Mr. Gulf said, clearing his throat. "We don't know exactly who saw Kevin." Even as he was saying the words, he knew that this was not sufficient evidence to suspend a student. Atticus could tell by the look on Mr. Gulf's face. But then, the jury that found Tom guilty knew only that Tom was black, and that was enough. "But we have enough evidence to know we've got the right boy," Mr. Gulf continued. "I appreciate your concern, but you'd best leave this matter to us. As I said, this isn't something you need to concern yourself with."

Trevor made a noise that Atticus ignored.

"But if you could just tell me who said he saw Kevin do it. Who wrote the note?" Atticus persisted.

"Atticus, please." Mr. Gulf was looking around, waving periodically to parents who wished him well.

"Was it a boy or a girl?" Atticus asked.

"I'm sorry," Mr. Gulf said in the middle of a new wave. "Atticus," he sighed deeply, "I appreciate your concern for a fellow classmate," Mr. Gulf started. "But I can assure you that a thorough investigation was conducted, and we feel very confident that Mr. Thurston, whom I might add had previously made it known just how he felt about Molly Vickers making the football team, is the guilty party." With that, he gave another abrupt wave to someone and was off, bidding the boys a good evening.

"I don't get you," Trevor said, breaking the

silence. "Why do you care about what happens to Kevin?"

" 'Cause he may not have done it."

"Yeah? And who did?"

"Someone from the Blendon football team," Atticus said. Even as he said it, they both sucked in some air. Trevor spoke first.

"What?" He sounded excited. "How do you know that?"

"Follow me," Atticus said.

"I always do," Trevor mused, pushing the chair at top speed.

•   •   •   •

It was strange to have Kevin Thurston in his house. It felt as though things in his life had shifted or been permanently altered by having this person come into his house and his room. But Atticus tried to act as if he didn't notice anything unusual about Kevin Thurston looking over his things. Trevor, however, was not so subtle. He scowled as Kevin looked over all the books and trophies on Atticus's bookcase.

"You got a lot of trophies," Kevin said in a surprised tone.

"Not exactly the kind of trophies you have, I know," Atticus said as he logged on to his computer.

Atticus had a dozen trophies—all academic. Most were from science fairs. One was for spelling. All were state championships. Trevor started to say something sarcastic, thought better of it, and snapped his mouth shut. Instead, he plopped himself down on Atticus's bed and continued to scowl. Trevor didn't like this. He didn't like this at all. Kevin was the enemy, and having him here, in one of their houses, just made Trevor uneasy.

"You read all these books?" Kevin asked, turning his head almost upside down reading all the titles.

"Yup," Atticus said. He had dialed up and was now getting onto the Internet.

"I haven't even heard of half of these," Kevin muttered.

Atticus heard Trevor choke back a sound from the bed.

"I've heard of this one," Kevin said, pulling out the *To Kill a Mockingbird* book. Mrs. Weaver had had it specially bound in a hard cover. It was a deep red with gold trim, making it look very elegant. It was Atticus's favorite book.

This distracted Atticus for just a moment, and he looked up from his computer to study Kevin's face.

"There's a smaller one next to it. Same book." Next to the large bound book was a small, old copy of the book. It was worn from being read and reread over the years. The front cover was torn slightly. Kevin pulled it out, examining it. "You can take it and read it sometime," Atticus said.

Another sound from Trevor, which everyone ignored.

"What do you have two copies of the same book for?"

"It's that good," Atticus muttered over his shoulder, returning to the computer. "Here it is."

Suddenly, all three boys were huddled around the computer reading the monitor. Atticus had pulled up the opinion poll of the local paper asking for readers' opinions of a girl football player.

"I hope it's not too late," Atticus muttered to himself. Often, a page was cleaned out to put in new comments.

"Here it is," Atticus said proudly, sitting back so Trevor and Kevin could read. "Without their star player (Kevin Thurston) playing . . ."

It was the entry from "Ticktock" that Atticus had remembered reading.

"So? Everyone's been saying that," Kevin

said in great confidence. "It's true, isn't it? We lost tonight."

Trevor made a face.

"Yes, but look at the date," Atticus reminded Kevin and Trevor. It was he who now sat back with an air of confidence, very proud of himself for having caught that.

"It's two days before Kevin was suspended," Trevor gasped.

Kevin dived forward again, rereading the entry.

"Hey! It is!" He looked at Atticus and back to the computer monitor again. "Who is this 'Ticktock' guy?"

"That's what we are going to find out," Atticus said, smiling smugly.

"Let me, let me," Trevor piped in, pushing Atticus's chair out of the way. This was exactly the kind of thing that Trevor loved to do on a computer. And, as the whole computer thing was still a little new to Atticus, he was glad to let Trevor do it. Plus, he was glad to see that Trevor was finally taking an interest in the idea of Kevin's innocence.

While Atticus and Kevin chatted politely, Trevor tapped into the member services section of the Internet. In the time that it took Trevor to track down the owner of the user name

"Ticktock," Atticus had tried the best he could to describe what the book *To Kill A Mockingbird* was about, why his mother named him Atticus, and how Boo Radley saved the day.

"Kinda like me," Kevin chimed in when Atticus explained the part about a man being falsely accused of crime he didn't commit.

"Gentlemen," Trevor spoke up, interrupting any hope Atticus had of getting Kevin Thurston interested in a classic like *To Kill a Mockingbird.* "Come meet Mr. Ticktock."

Kevin pounced. Atticus had to wiggle his way in between Trevor and Kevin to read the name on the screen. Stephen and Caroline Williams.

They all blinked.

"Who are Stephen and Caroline Williams?" Trevor asked.

"Check my backpack." Atticus pointed Trevor toward the pack on the back of his chair. "We still have that game roster. We can check for the name *Williams*," Atticus said. His thinking was they would find a Blendon player with the name Williams.

"You don't need to," Kevin said suddenly and both boys looked at him. "Stephen and Caroline are his parents."

"Whose?" both boys asked.

"Martin Williams." Kevin's voice was grave. "He plays on the Blendon team. He used to be one of my best friends."

Atticus and Trevor both looked at each other and then back at Kevin Thurston. Atticus could feel his pulse racing again. They had found "Ticktock"—the letter writer.

"This guy used to be your friend?" Trevor squeaked. "Some friend."

"Used to be. When we were little, we used to play on the same little league team. Me, Kyle Patrick, Connor Pearson, Martin, lots of us. All of our parents used to hang out, you know, do the barbecue thing and all that. We won our division one year," Kevin remembered, still staring at the name on the monitor. "We were in the fourth grade or something like that. Then his family moved. I haven't seen him much. He's been around. I just haven't seen him. We run in different circles, you know? Then last year I saw him at a game. We said, you know, 'Hi, how's it going?' "

"Yeah, I guess you guys were pretty good friends then," Trevor muttered. Kevin turned, scowling at Trevor.

"Hey, good enough that I never would have thought he'd do something like this." Even as he said it, Kevin shook his head in disbelief. "I would've never believed he'd do something like this."

"So, what are we saying here?" Trevor asked, just wanting to make sure he understood what Atticus was thinking. "This guy, Martin, put the letter in Molly's locker? That he's the one who made the drawings all over her picture and stuck it up on the wall over her locker? Well," he said, spreading his hands out, palms up, "how do you think he did that? It was during the day, remember? He was in school. *His* school. Are you saying that you think he came clear across town to another school to do all that to Molly's locker? How did he get here? Don't you think someone might have recognized him? Don't you think someone would have remembered a guy like him walking around the school hallways?"

As Trevor asked these questions, Atticus was suddenly filled with some of his own. Even if Martin Williams had somehow made it all the way across town into Walnut Middle School without anyone noticing him, how had he known which locker was Molly's? And Trevor had been right. It was an awfully big risk. He shook his head as he thought about it. It didn't make sense.

"Then how do you explain this statement?" Atticus asked, thumping the monitor screen with his knuckle. "How do you explain this Martin guy saying that Kevin was off the team when he wasn't? How do you explain that unless—"

Before Atticus could finish, Trevor cut him off. "Maybe he was saying it like, *if* Kevin Thurston was gone then the Walnut Cougars would be nothing. Like that."

Kevin nodded to this. "I agree with Trey."

"It's Trevor," Trevor growled at Kevin.

"What? Oh, yeah. Sorry."

Atticus shook his head slowly.

"I don't know," he started.

"It's not that I don't appreciate what you're trying to do," Kevin started, picking up his jacket. "But I think you got the wrong guy. He couldn't have done it. It had to be someone from our own school."

"Look," Atticus reasoned, "this guy had a reason. With you off the team, he could make sure Blendon won, right?"

"Well, if you look at it that way, it could have been anyone from any of the schools we play. There are a lot of guys who'd like to see me gone," Kevin said flatly. He shrugged his shoulders at Atticus. "Sorry, I just don't see it happening like you say." With that, Kevin gave a wave and ducked out the door.

"Do you believe that guy?" Trevor said in astonishment. "He called me *Trey*. The guy's been chasing me around for the last year trying to kill me, and he thinks my name is Trey!"

"He knows your name," Atticus said mildly, still staring at the computer screen. "He was just trying to rile you up."

"Man, I can't believe that guy. You're trying to help him, and he can't be bothered." Trevor stomped around the room for a couple of minutes. "You know, he probably did it. He probably did it and was hoping you could pin it on someone else, but you couldn't."

"He didn't do it."

"That's the only reason he came over here, I bet. To see if you could pin it on someone else. But you can't. He did it. I bet ya he did it," said Trevor, still seething from being called Trey.

"He didn't do it, I tell ya," Atticus shot back.

"How do you know?" Trevor laughed, but he was not happy. It was the kind of laugh he gave when he was getting mad. "He can't even remember other people's names. All he cares about is himself, and I don't get you trying to clear his name."

But Atticus had seen the way Kevin looked when Molly had taken a hit. He had heard the way Kevin called out. And, even here in his own room, he had seen the way Kevin was looking at the books, the way he was listening to Atticus while he explained the story *To Kill a Mockingbird*. There was more to Kevin Thurston than just being some big, tough jock. Atticus was sure.

"I gotta go home," Trevor said finally in utter frustration. Atticus barely heard him. Trevor called out to Mrs. Weaver to let her know that he was going.

Atticus continued to stare at the screen. It was difficult to explain, but he had heard the way that number 76, Martin Williams, talked to his teammates as he trotted past Atticus at halftime.

What was it he said?

Tick tock! Tick tock!

It had been the *way* he had said it. It was the way guys share a joke, thinking that no one else will get what they are saying. He had said it as though it were an inside joke, and the others had laughed too.

Could he be wrong? Maybe he was just reading into things.

Atticus sighed, shutting down the computer. Maybe . . . As he moved closer to his bed, preparing to get in it, he noticed the smaller book he had suggested Kevin Thurston should read was gone.

He turned off the light, smiling to himself. He hadn't been wrong.

THE DANCE

In the following week, Atticus spoke to every teacher he could think of, but no one could remember who specifically he or she had allowed to walk the halls the day Molly's locker was "decorated." And no one could remember seeing anyone strange in the hallways. Atticus spoke to the janitors and Ms. North, the school secretary. There was nothing unusual.

Trevor was disgusted by all of this and had very little to do with Atticus while he played detective. With no clues and no Trevor, the only highlight of the week had been that Kevin Thurston was no longer interested in chasing Trevor and Atticus around. Atticus supposed that while he wasn't able to clear Kevin's name from the crime, there was a part of Kevin that truly appreciated what he was trying to do.

Atticus had thought about telling Trevor how Kevin had taken the copy of *To Kill a Mockingbird* but changed his mind. Trevor would probably just say Kevin stole it to be mean or was using it as a doorstop or something. So Trevor went right on fuming about the fact that Kevin had called him Trey and declaring that Atticus was wasting his time by talking to all the teachers. And Atticus kept on talking to the teachers, hoping to come across something he hadn't seen or thought of before.

The end of the week wasn't much of an improvement either, as Walnut lost to the Sunbury Tigers 17 to 23. Molly Vickers was awesome, but it wasn't enough to make a win for the Cougars. Without Kevin Thurston, there was a real gap in the team. Just as with the previous week, the Cougar fans left the bleachers with their heads hanging low. Everyone, that is, except Amy Loe. Atticus and Trevor watched as she ran around with the cheerleaders from the other school.

"She knows everyone," Trevor said, rolling his eyes. They could hear her telling some kind of joke clear across the field.

"Yeah, I think she goes to some kind of cheerleading camp every summer. They all know one another," Atticus explained. He had heard her talking about it before. Amy Loe was the kind of person who talked especially loud so that everyone around her would know exactly what she had done the past weekend, where she had gone, who she had seen, and how much fun she had had. She was very clear about that. She always liked people to know how much fun she had.

Atticus frowned for a moment, popping a Junior Mint into his mouth.

"What?" Trevor caught his expression.

"Amy," was all Atticus said, still watching her.

"Yeah?"

"She knows everyone."

"Uh huh."

"And everyone knows her."

"They'd have to," Trevor shrugged. "She's too loud to miss."

"Even the Blendon cheerleaders."

Trevor groaned. "Are you on that again?"

Atticus had never left it. It was something that he thought about night and day. He just couldn't shake the sound of Martin Williams' voice when he'd said, "Tick tock. Tick tock."

But even as Trevor complained about it, he began gradually pushing Atticus through the gate to the field and onto the track toward the cheerleaders. Atticus said nothing but continued to watch Amy Loe and munch on his Junior Mints.

"I don't even know my routine yet." Amy was talking to three other girls Atticus did not know. "I'm gonna learn it this weekend."

"You better," one of the other girls giggled. "Or you're going to look stupid at the competition."

"No, she's gonna learn it," another girl said, throwing an arm over Amy's shoulder and pretending to show Amy a fist. "Or else."

"I'll get it! I'll get it!" Amy assured her.

"Okay, so next Saturday," the girl with the fist said.

"Yup!" Amy nodded. The other girls waved and started to run off. Amy caught Atticus and Trevor's glance and gave them a curious smile, no doubt wondering why they were coming toward her.

"You sure know a lot of people," Atticus started slowly.

"Yeah."

"How do you know so many people from other schools? I saw you talking to a bunch of the cheerleaders at last week's game too." Atticus said. Amy smiled and shrugged. It was no secret.

"We all cheer together. Well, some of us. Some I know from cheerleading camp. But, like those girls I was just talking to, we all cheer together at AmeriCheer. It's a club."

Trevor and Atticus exchanged glances.

"So, do you cheer with some girls from Blendon?"

"Yeah." Amy furrowed her brows at them. "Why?" Then she got a slow grin. "You like someone?"

Trevor started to make a sound, but Atticus hit his arm. Trevor quickly withdrew it, holding it but saying nothing more.

"Maybe. Or maybe some of the players or cheerleaders know something about Kevin Thurston's suspension from school," he said slowly.

Amy's eyes flew wide open, and she hopped closer to them, clasping her hands together.

"Who? Who?"

If there was one thing Amy Loe liked, it was being on the inside of a secret. If there was one thing Amy Loe couldn't do, it was keep a secret. For this reason, Atticus decided to pace himself. Maybe he could tell her just enough that she might offer up some names. He had no idea where this might take him, but he had asked all the teachers everything he could think of and no one could give him any answers. Now, suddenly, Amy Loe seemed like a possible link between Blendon and Walnut. She knew everyone, and it was very likely, given her ability to talk (at top volume), that she could have told someone where Molly's locker was. Specifically, she could have told a cheerleader who was asking on behalf of Martin Williams.

Atticus got excited by this idea. Perhaps a cheerleader from Blendon fell into conversation with Amy Loe, and somehow Molly Vicker's name came up. This would be very likely as Molly had had an article written about her and many people were wondering about her. Amy Loe would have been more than happy to provide all the inside information to anyone who asked. Without thinking, she would even tell the enemy camp all about Walnut's newest weapon.

"What are you saying?" she asked, narrowing her eyes at him.

But before Atticus could explain any further, there was a very Amylike voice shouting out her name. This was, he decided, for the best because he needed to put more thought into how he could use Amy.

"Yo! Amy!" a voice boomed out over the field. Trevor, Atticus, and Amy all looked up to see a large barrel-chested man calling to her. Amy was built just like him. They were both thick and powerful looking with wild hair and wide mouths. "Come on, babeee! We gotta hustle! Come onnnnn!"

"Amy's father," Trevor and Atticus said to each other at the same time. This surprised Amy for a moment, as though she wondered how they could have possibly guessed that.

"Okay!" she bellowed back. "We'll talk later," she said, hitting Atticus on the arm and hurrying off.

"What was that about?" Trevor asked, and Atticus shared his thoughts with his friend.

"So, maybe that's our lead," he finished up, popping the last Junior Mint into his mouth. "Maybe Martin Williams has a partner in crime."

"Are you sure you didn't say too much? You know Amy's going to talk about this to everyone," Trevor pointed out.

"Maybe that's the best way to get this thing started," Atticus said.

Atticus had the scenario all worked out in his mind. Just how Martin Williams got to their school, he was not so sure. But, once inside, it was probably easy enough to act. He probably wore a baseball cap pulled down low over his eyebrows so no one would recognize him. With the locker number given to him by way of Amy Loe, Martin made his way through the school. He probably looked around, making sure no one saw him. It was right in the middle of classes, so everyone else was safely out of sight.

Once the coast was clear, Martin just slipped the note into Molly's locker, easy as pie, and ran out of the school without anyone thinking anything of it. It could have been that easy. In fact, it could have been so easy, this Martin character could have had anyone do it.

"So, what now? You're going to find this Martin guy and get him to confess?" Trevor asked skeptically. "He'll squash you like a bug."

"No, but maybe I could . . ." His voice trailed off. "Maybe I could do something; I don't know yet. I haven't had time to work it out."

"Yeah, well, you just told Amy Loe you think someone from Blendon is in on all of this. You'd better think fast, because knowing her, you don't have much time."

He would have to think of something clever but simple. It was like in the scene with Atticus Finch when he stood in the courtroom trying to prove how Tom couldn't have used his left hand to commit the crime. Atticus Finch was interviewing the witness who had accused him of the crime. Suddenly he asked Tom to stand up. He asked, "Is this the man who did it?" Atticus said he wanted Tom's accuser to have good, hard look at him. But really, the reason Atticus Finch had Tom stand up was so the jury could see Tom's arm. His left arm was a foot shorter than his right arm. His left hand was shriveled, and it was obvious that his left arm had no use. There was no way Tom could have committed the crime. It was a pivotal moment in the case. That was what Atticus Weaver needed. Something . . . well, something pivotal.

Another week passed, and nothing major happened. It was a funny thing about pivotal moments. Atticus wasn't sure if one had come along and he just hadn't noticed it. Much of the week had been the same. Kevin Thurston had been leaving both Trevor and Atticus alone, as were his friends, until the end of the week. Then suddenly, in a life-threatening moment, Atticus noticed a change. It was subtle, it was hardly noticeable but, then, there it was. And conceivably, that little discovery was the beginning of his hero status. It wasn't the *beginning* of the beginning, but it was the beginning of Atticus discovering who he really was. Still, at the time, it didn't seem nearly so important. In fact, Atticus was hardly aware of it, but perhaps that was because of Molly Vickers.

Atticus had not seen much of Kevin Thurston. In fact, no one had seen much of him. Without his football hero status, Kevin had become rather quiet. He was no longer the leader of the Cougar team. He was no longer the leader of his bully friends. He seemed to have kind of faded into the background. Kyle Patrick was the new quarterback, the new team leader. Things seemed to be changing everywhere.

• • • •

With the ring of the final bell, Thursday had proven to be a day just like every other day. Except for the fact that everyone was talking about the big dance coming up. But that kind of thing never affected Trevor or Atticus one way or the other, so for them it was like any other day. Trevor and Atticus went to each other's lockers, collected various books and homework assignments, and prepared to leave school. They headed for the gym, hoping to cut through to get to the other side of the school, when they heard someone call out their names. Both Trevor and Atticus looked behind them to find the fair Molly Vickers running to catch up with them. Trevor had just put his hand on the gymnasium door, ready to open it, when she called out. Now he stood motionless, letting his hand fall back to his side. *Molly Vickers! What could she want with them?!*

Atticus blinked. She was coming at an almost slow-motion pace. He could see every detail of her. She was trying to keep her backpack over her left shoulder, causing her to lean out to the right. This made all her hair tumble over to the side, flowing around her like a golden cloud. She was beautiful.

His heart skipped a beat.

"Atticus! Wait!" she said again, but there was no need. Not an earthquake or a hurricane could move him from this spot. He sat speechless as she came closer.

When she was only two feet from them, she relaxed and smiled, relieved to have caught them.

"Whew! I didn't think I would find you." She laughed and looked from Trevor to Atticus. "You guys always get out of here so fast."

Both Trevor and Atticus just stared at her.

She was beautiful. What could she want with them?

She's talking to us.

She knows our names.

Her smiled faded a little as they both stared, stupefied, at her.

"Okay, well, anyway, I wanted to talk to you for a minute."

Stare.

"Um, I wanted to ask you . . ." She fidgeted with her backpack. For one delirious moment, Atticus thought she might be trying to ask him to the dance. It was insane, but hanging over her head was a banner for the upcoming dance. She looked around nervously to make sure no one was around. It was all anyone was talking about. Who was going to go with whom . . .

"I heard from Amy Loe that you guys don't think that Kevin Thurston, you know, did what he did. You don't think he did it?"

As soon as she said it, she kind of laughed again nervously. Atticus felt his face flush. How stupid could he be? As if a girl like Molly Vickers was ever going to ask a guy like *him* to the dance. As if he could dance. What a dope!

"He didn't do it," Atticus said abruptly. Both Trevor and Molly gave a look of surprise as he said this. He couldn't say exactly why, but he felt very strongly about the fact that Kevin Thurston had not betrayed Molly Vickers in the way everyone thought he had. Perhaps because he was so irritated with himself for having such a foolish idea come into his head or just because he was sick of this subject. He had been her friend and hadn't wanted to see her get hurt. They used to walk to class together. They used to go to dances together. He had liked her. He had liked her a lot. Maybe he didn't want her to play football, but he sure wouldn't do anything mean to her. Atticus had seen the expression on Kevin's face when he thought she was hurt. He couldn't have pretended that. But Atticus couldn't prove any of this. And he couldn't get anyone else to listen to him. And the whole thing, including the fact that he was a nobody and would never be asked to the dance by the most beautiful girl in the school, was very, very upsetting to him.

"How do you know?" Molly recovered.

"Because I just know it. Only I haven't figured out how to prove it yet."

They all stared at one another for a moment.

"Haven't you talked to him yourself?" Atticus suddenly wondered. "What does he say to you?"

"I haven't talked to him," she stated. "He's tried." She shrugged her shoulders. "But I haven't listened." She looked a little embarrassed about this. Then she furrowed her brows. "You really don't think he did it?" she said, leaning in.

Locks of golden hair fell forward, and her big blues eyes were fastened tightly on his. Atticus swallowed, but he wasn't admiring Molly at that moment. He was so mad at himself about how goofy he had been. Beauties don't ask outcasts to a dance. This was one of the sure things in life. There were laws of physics, and there were laws of school cliques. Some things never change.

"No."

"Then, who?" she wanted to know, now more curious than ever. In better times, this quizzical look could have been rather appealing, but Atticus Weaver was like a rock now.

"Don't know. Maybe someone from Blendon."

"Blendon?" She was astonished. "But why would someone from Blendon . . .?" She stopped herself. The idea that people objected so powerfully to a girl playing football was still a very upsetting idea for her. She bit her lower lip, staring at the boys.

"It probably doesn't have anything to do with you," Atticus said quickly, reading her mind.

"Nothing to do with me?" She laughed out loud at this, and her voice rose, echoing off the walls. They were all alone. There were faraway voices as the kids trailed out of the school from the front exits. "I got that letter in my locker! How do you figure that's got nothing to do with me? It had my name on it."

"It was a diversion," Atticus said.

"A what?" She threw a wild look to Trevor, who just shrugged his shoulders at her. "People saw him walking around in the hallways before I got it. He was walking around my locker that morning when he, when someone, put that picture of me up on the wall."

"People? Like who?" Atticus wanted to know.

"Like Kyle Patrick and Amy Loe for one," she said.

"That's two," Trevor helped out. Molly ignored him.

"They didn't want to get Kevin in trouble, but they saw him out walking around in the hallways."

"How is it that Amy Loe always knows what's going on?" Trevor asked out loud to no one in particular.

"How did they see Kevin? Were they out in the halls?" Atticus asked. Why was it no one knew that they were in the halls as well?

"Hey, Molly!" A voice boomed down the hallway, and the trio saw Amy Loe waving at them from the distance. "I heard Kyle Patrick asked you to the dance!" With that, Amy gave Molly a thumbs-up, waved, and disappeared. Molly made a small giggling sound, and Atticus's heart sank.

He could adjust to most things. It's what he had done all his life. And adjusting to the idea that a girl like Molly Vickers would never ask a boy like Atticus Weaver to the dance was easy enough. He could handle that. But he did not like the idea of her going with another boy, one he did not particularly like, at all. He gritted his teeth and pretended not to have heard any of that.

Molly turned her attention back to Atticus and shrugged. "I think Amy was showing something to Kyle or they were late to class or something. I don't know. But they saw Kevin."

Atticus nodded at this. It was entirely possible that Kyle and Amy also saw someone else but didn't think anything of it. After all, it was Kevin who had the reputation of wanting Molly off the team. It was Kevin who had talked to the reporter and told him that having Molly on the team was a bad thing.

"Well," Molly said, readjusting her backpack. "I was just wondering. I heard people talking about it and thought I would ask you. I hope you're right."

"What are people saying about it?" Trevor asked her as she was about to leave. "About what Atticus thinks?"

Molly got a pained looked on her face and screwed up her lips as though she was fighting to keep the words from coming out of her mouth.

"What?" Trevor asked again, impatiently.

"That you guys are doing this just to get on his good side so he won't, you know, chase you anymore." Then she turned to Trevor, and Trevor only, and said, "Or beat *you* up." Atticus fell back into his chair. With that, she was off, leaving Atticus to stare after her. A girl like her would never ask a guy like him to the dance. He didn't like it, but he could accept it. For one thing, he couldn't exactly dance. But he couldn't even get himself beat up. He had called Kevin Thurston dumb in front of the whole school, and would Kevin throw a punch? Not even. Instead, he called Atticus a cripple. That had been bad enough. But when Atticus was able to forgive Kevin and maybe help him out of a jam, no one could believe that a kid like Kevin could be friends with a kid like Atticus. So everyone had to believe that Atticus was helping Kevin because he was some kind of a wimp, a baby, a chicken.

Atticus could feel heat rising up to the tops of his ears—something that only happened when he was really mad. He wasn't afraid of being hit! That was the exact thing he wasn't afraid of. Couldn't everyone see that? Couldn't they see that the one thing he had loads of was courage? Couldn't they see past the chair and the glasses?

"Come on," Trevor had muttered, turning them into the gym, but Atticus barely heard him. His mind was reeling. He was angry. He was upset. He couldn't even get himself beat up if he wanted to!

Ker-slam!

The heavy gym doors slapped shut behind them, snapping Atticus back to attention. Both Atticus and Trevor turned to see Connor Pearson, Jeff Borden, and David Lepac standing against the walls, arms folded against their chests, smiling. It wasn't a "Hi! Glad to see ya" smile. More like the way a hungry cat would look at a big fat mouse.

"Oh, man," Trevor groaned beneath his breath. Trapped! Trevor took one stride forward, starting to give Atticus's chair a good push when they saw Kyle Patrick and Cameron Norris on the other side of the gym, blocking off their exit.

"Look, it's Sherlock Holmes," one of the boys scoffed. "Hey, Detective Weaver? What clues have you come up with?"

If Atticus Weaver were later asked to name the specific time and place in his life that he decided that enough was enough, if there had been a time when he could say that he rebelled against the clique system, this was it. What he had felt in the parking lot was nothing compared to how he felt now.

By all accounts, the Walnut football players had only wanted to ask him about what clues he had turned up in the Kevin Thurston case. Unlikely, but possible. Still, neither Trevor nor Atticus would ever find out.

The Dance

"You guys suck!" Atticus hurled the insult so loudly and so violently that everyone stood stock-still for several moments. No one had ever spoken to them that way before. Then Atticus heard Trevor wheezing. But Atticus didn't care.

"You guys are the worst. The only reason you even had a score on the board was 'cause of Molly. A girl! She's saving your butts! You guys stink!"

"ARE YOU INSANE?" Trevor asked as he began dancing around the back of the chair. There was no place to go, no place to run.

Someone yelled to get them, and there was the sudden charge of all the football players. There were five doors to the giant gymnasium. Two exits from the school side—the doors they had come through—and two more across the gym floor that led out to the back of the school. On the home-side of the bleachers was one more door that led down the hallway toward the locker rooms. Trevor began running toward that door, but Kyle and Cameron saw where they were headed and ran back to cut across the floor.

"Get him!" Kyle shouted.

"They're cutting across."

Trevor planted the balls of his feet on the floor, pushing off as hard as he could, but it was no use. Kyle was cutting them off before Trevor could get enough speed behind the chair.

Seeing him, Trevor tugged hard on the right side of the chair and turned them to the right, cutting past Cameron, who came to a skidding halt. As big as Cameron was, he was not able to turn as quickly, and Trevor and Atticus were flying toward one of the back doors. But Connor and David Lepac were running straight at them from the other side. Trevor knew even if he got to the door first, he wouldn't have enough time to open it and get Atticus through. This wasn't a game of tag.

Again, Trevor cut hard on the chair, popping a side wheelie and flying out toward the middle of the gym floor. Around and around they went, with the players calling after them. Their voices echoed off the walls. To anyone outside, it might have sounded like a rousing game of basketball. How could anyone know that they were running for their lives?

Running for their lives!

Atticus could only hope. But, just to be doubly sure . . .

"You guys suck!" he screamed from his chair as Trevor narrowly maneuvered them out of the reach of Connor Pearson.

"Ha ha! Missed, you big ape!" Atticus hollered over his shoulder. Trevor was marking up the floor with wheel marks as he jerked the chair left and right.

"Shut up!" Trevor screeched at Atticus, but Atticus was beside himself. His arms were flailing about as he was pointing fingers and taunting the other boys.

Trevor and Atticus made four more laps of the gym with the boys running behind them, threatening them. Trevor had truly mastered the art of dodging and weaving, making it impossible for anyone to get hold of them. He did have, after all, over a year's training from pushing the wheelchair while running through the schoolyard and neighborhoods. If he kept this up much longer, he was sure he would be able to try out for the U.S. bobsled team! Everyone was beginning to tire.

Panting and wheezing, Trevor tried a new tactic, charging the other boys with Atticus's chair to get them to back off. Kyle, Cameron, and David were on one side, closest to the locker room door. Connor, the linebacker, was doubled over at the waist, trying to catch his breath. With his hands resting on the tops of his thighs, he craned his head up to see what was going on. Trevor doubled back, moving around Connor as though he were going to go back to the far back doors. This drew Jeff Borden over, thinking he was going to block them off. Then, with a brilliant tug to the side, Trevor and Atticus sideswiped Jeff, bolted passed Connor, who was still unable to move, and headed for the front double doors.

The gymnasium was alive with everyone yelling. If one didn't know better, it would have sounded like an entire high school was in the gym cheering for their team. But these guys were threatening serious bodily harm! Then, Atticus heard a thud. More of a slapping sound, actually. But it hadn't mattered. They were flying. The chair felt so light. They were cruising at what seemed to be 100 miles per hour. *Use your hands.*

"Whooo—ee!" Atticus yelled, just to further taunt the other players. Trevor had never run so fast.

Suddenly, strangely, Atticus realized how very quiet the gym had become. *Use your hands.*

"Okay, that's good," Atticus half laughed, half warned. They were coming dangerously close to the double doors and showing no sign of slowing.

"Use your hands!"

Atticus turned to warn Trevor off when he realized that it was Trevor's voice he had been hearing. *Use your hands.* He turned to look behind him only to find that there was no one there. No Trevor. Trevor was on the floor. Horror flooded Atticus.

The Dance

Kyle, Cameron, Connor, David, Jeff, and Trevor all stared at Atticus. There was nothing anyone else could do but watch as Atticus flew into the doors at top speed. There was no time to retrieve his gloves from his backpack. Atticus turned and faced the oncoming walls.

Trevor had tripped or been tripped, hitting the floor hard, and could only watch as his best friend helplessly soared into a wall.

Gritting his teeth, Atticus tried to grab the tops of his wheels, but it was no use. Even the little bit that he had grabbed mangled his hands. Instinctively, he pulled them back. A moment later, he crashed into the corner of the wall and part of the door.

It was a sickening sound. For a moment, all Atticus could see was blackness. He felt his body crumple against the door with the hard impact. Thankfully, the door gave, making a loud explosion sound. Atticus's chair burst through the door but then skidded to a stop and dumped him over. Lying halfway in and halfway out of the gym, Atticus was motionless for a moment.

Books, pens, and papers flew out from the capsized chair, and one wheel spun around and around as though it were still traveling along at top speed. It fanned Atticus as he lay on the floor in a groaning, pathetic heap.

"Oh, man!" he heard one of the boys say as they approached. For a moment, he saw that Jeff Borden was looking down at him to make sure he was okay. Then Jeff laughed along with the others and just stepped over him and his chair.

"Oh, that's gotta hurt!"

"Hey, that's some good driving, Smith," someone called over his shoulder to Trevor, who was crawling forward trying to reach his friend.

More laughter.

Atticus could feel parts of his body throbbing. Still, yet again, no one had laid a finger on him.

"You still stink," he called out after them as they disappeared into the halls.

THE PLAY

"**WHAT** happened?" Mrs. Weaver gasped when she saw Atticus and Trevor come through the door. The wheelchair, for the most part, was intact. One of the wheels was bent out of shape a little, but it was still functional and could be easily fixed. The same could not be said of Atticus.

"Oh, honey, what happened?" She had had the day's mail in her hand, going through the bills, when she saw the condition of her son and let the letters fall to the floor. Atticus had a slight cut on his forehead, and blood was streaming down the side of his head. While the head injury was very mild, the blood made it seem far worse, and Mrs. Weaver had to be consoled by Atticus.

"Mom! Mom, it's nothing. It doesn't even hurt," he was saying. "It's a scratch. I think I scratched it on the side of the chair." Just *how* he did that, Atticus was not going to share with her.

"Yeah, I bet his legs are way worse," Trevor helped out, and Atticus hissed at him. Mrs. Weaver looked up, startled.

"Someone please tell me what happened!"

Trevor did. Before Atticus could cut him off, Trevor explained how he had tried to outmaneuver the guy, but Connor had managed to reach forward and grab hold of his leg, tripping him. Trevor had landed hard, leaving Atticus to fend for himself. With that, Trevor was apologizing for the fiftieth time since they had left the school, saying how he had sworn he would never let that kind of thing happen again, and he had. But this time, it truly was not his fault. Atticus tried to explain this to him. It was Atticus who had picked the fight, calling those goons names. It was Atticus who had been looking for trouble. Not Trevor.

"You didn't do it," Atticus sighed. "Trev, forget it. It wasn't you. Connor grabbed your leg."

But Trevor could not be consoled. And neither could Mrs. Weaver, who was up and moving toward the phone ready to call the school.

"Who is this Connor person?" she demanded.

"Besides, if I hadn't started it," Atticus was still saying to Trevor. He looked over at his mother. "I started it, Mom," he said.

"You?" Her mouth fell open.

"Yeah, so please put the phone back." Atticus waved a hand at her. The last thing he needed or wanted was for his mother to call the school and complain.

"What's going on?" she said, still shaking her head, unable to believe that her son would start some kind of fight.

"Mom, just put the phone down."

"I'll do no such thing. I want to find out what kind of boy fights with a boy in . . ." She stopped herself for a moment. "I'm not going to let this slide, Atticus," she huffed.

"What, Mom? Fights a cripple? Is that what you were going to say?" Atticus roared, and she looked shocked. Trevor dropped his head for a minute. "That was what you were thinking, wasn't it? Just like everyone else, and I'm sick of it." But Mrs. Weaver was shaking her head.

"You know better than that, Atticus. You know better than that! But, yes, I am appalled to think that there is a boy out there who would fight with another boy in a wheelchair. It's not a fair fight. And there is no shame in that!" She waved a finger at him.

"But I started this," he said, calming a little bit.

"Why? Why would you do something like that? Who is this Connor boy?" she asked again, this time looking to Trevor for a little help.

"It's true, Mrs. Weaver, he did start it. Today." Trevor leaned forward with that and hit his friend in the arm. "But it's been going on for a long time. Way before today. And it's not about Connor Pearson. It doesn't even have anything to do with him, really."

"Then who? Tell me what's going on," she said. Trevor and Atticus exchanged glances. "Or else, I call." She taunted them with the telephone. Atticus nodded gravely. "From the beginning," she warned. "Just start from the beginning."

And so it was that Atticus would have to start from the very beginning to explain how it had come to be that he was banged up in a one-chair accident. And why Atticus Weaver, of all people, would start a fight. So he started from the very beginning as best as he could recall it. Still, it was troublesome. It is difficult to start from the beginning when you don't have an ending.

Bit by bit, he pieced the entire story together for his mother. He told her how Molly had made the team and how the Blendon football player had made the remark about Kevin Thurston not being on the team days before he was actually kicked off. "So that's why you had him over here the other day?" Mrs. Weaver thought out loud. Atticus nodded.

"Yeah, a lot of good it did us," Trevor mused.

"He didn't even appreciate what we were trying to do. He even claims that we were doing it just to get in with the popular crowd." Trevor made a face when he said the word *popular*. "Like I want to hang out with them!" He snorted to himself. "He couldn't even remember my name."

Atticus looked at Trevor for a minute.

"When was the last time you saw Kevin hanging out with the football gang?" he asked suddenly. Trevor thought about this for a moment and shrugged his shoulders.

"I don't know. It's been a while. They don't hang out with him now that he's not the star quarterback!" Trevor made another face at Mrs. Weaver. "See, that's how great of a bunch of friends they all are. The second you aren't the star, they drop you like a hot potato."

"Yeah, so why do they care if we are being all buddy-buddy with Kevin?" Atticus asked.

"We aren't."

"Yeah, but that's what they're saying, right? And I'm asking, why do they care if they aren't friends with him anymore?" Atticus raised his eyebrows at his friend. Trevor pondered this for a moment.

"I don't know," Trevor said slowly. "Kyle's the big star now. I don't know why he even cares."

"Who's Kyle?" Mrs. Weaver asked. While

Atticus explained all the characters in this complicated story, Mrs. Weaver got a cold washcloth to clean up Atticus's forehead. He grimaced as she cleaned him up, mostly embarrassed that Trevor would see it, but continued with his explanation.

With Kevin Thurston out of the picture, Kyle Patrick became the new quarterback for the Cougars. Only, he just wasn't as good as Kevin, so the Cougars were not doing so well. This was pretty upsetting to the rest of the school.

No one was mad at Kyle. They knew that he was trying his best. Maybe that was why he was so popular. He was seen as the guy who was trying to help out. Everyone was mad at Kevin. He was the guy who let everyone down by doing such a mean and stupid thing to Molly. But the question that Atticus had been asking all along was . . . had he really? Had Kevin Thurston let everyone down? Atticus didn't think so. Kevin had too much to lose by getting kicked off the team, being disliked by his fellow classmates, letting the Cougars lose, and hurting Molly.

"But someone else had a lot to gain," Atticus said out loud.

Both Mrs. Weaver and Trevor stared at Atticus for a moment. He rolled his eyes impatiently, answering his own question.

"Who is the starting quarterback now because Kevin is gone? And who is suddenly super popular? Who had easy access to Molly's locker early in the morning? Who refused to talk to the press but stood right beside Kevin when he did all the talking, making it easy for Kevin to look like the bad guy? Who got Molly to go to the dance with him, and *who* was seen walking around in the hallways when Kevin supposedly put the letter in Molly's locker?"

"I thought you said it was that Martin guy from Blendon," Trevor sighed.

"I did. And he definitely knew about it all." Atticus chewed on his finger for a minute. Then in a stroke of genius, it was Trevor who snapped his fingers and added the final piece to the puzzle.

"Didn't Kevin say that he and Kyle and Martin Williams all played together? Isn't that what he said?" Trevor turned to Mrs. Weaver to include her in what was going on. "Kevin told us that when they were in little league, he and Kyle and this other guy named Martin Williams all played together. Then Martin moved away. Kevin didn't see him anymore, but Kyle did!"

Atticus could have kissed him. Only, that wasn't the kind of thing you did with your best buddy. Instead, he offered a big, toothy grin.

"That's right! He did." He looked back and forth between his mother and Trevor. "We've got him now. Now we just have to prove it!"

•   •   •   •

Atticus needed to do something spectacular now. Just like when Atticus Finch asked Tom to stand up in the courtroom. Atticus Weaver needed that pivotal point. He couldn't very well ask Kyle Patrick to stand up. For one thing, he wasn't at all sure what that would accomplish, and for another, Kyle was very much in control of both arms. Although, some people didn't think his throwing arm was all that accurate.

Trevor and Atticus had been hard at work, eating pretzels for brainpower, trying to think of how to catch Kyle Patrick. "Perhaps I could make a suggestion," Mrs. Weaver cut in. "I think Molly Vickers is your answer," she said.

Atticus knew his mom was right. Why hadn't he thought of Molly? Well, actually, he always thought of Molly. Just not this time for the right reason. But Molly was the answer. She held the power. She was the school sweetheart. She was the dream girl. She was the girl who packed in all the geeks, freaks, outcasts, and jocks to the pep rallies and football games. Still, she had more power in her little pinky than any Kyle Patrick or Kevin Thurston could ever have and had nary a clue about it. That was about to change.

With a mere phone call, Atticus and Trevor were able to convince Molly that she needed to come over to their house to talk. It was something, they assured her, that could not be discussed in school. They could not risk anyone seeing them together. They couldn't risk jeopardizing the plan in any way. All of this, of course, had been enough to pique Molly's interest. She had asked over and over again what it was they wanted to talk about.

"It's about Kevin Thurston and how to prove he's innocent. But you can't tell anyone you're coming over here. Not anyone, because you'll just never believe who your *real* enemy is!"

When Atticus hung up the phone, he turned to Trevor and his mother, who were both staring wide-eyed at him.

"Well?"

"She's coming right over," Atticus breathed. Molly Vickers. Here, in his very own house. He could feel a sweat coming on. The presence of Kevin Thurston had been powerful enough. Having Molly Vickers over was going to change things forever.

"Oh, good." Mrs. Weaver clasped her hands together. "I'll make something. How about that? I'll make something for you guys to munch on while you . . ."

Atticus flushed. This was his opportunity to show how cool he really was. This was his chance to have Molly Vickers on his turf, his terms. He could show her how smart, how clever, how nice, and how cool he was. But having his mother around offering homemade chocolate chip cookies was not the way to do it. He looked down in his lap for a moment and then cleared his throat.

"Do you, um, do you think you could run some errands or something?" he asked. Her face fell for a moment. She looked over at Trevor, who quickly and respectfully looked down to examine his shoelaces. She looked back to Atticus.

"Well, sure," she said and shrugged. "I guess I could run out for a couple of minutes and get us . . ." She thought for a minute. "I could go to McDonald's and get us some dinner. Trevor, would you like to eat over here tonight? The fries are on me." She managed a weak smile, and Atticus felt momentarily guilty. She was a good mom. But he just couldn't risk blowing his only chance. He just couldn't see too many other times in his life when he would have Molly Vickers in his house.

"I'll ask my mom," Trevor said, reaching for the phone.

"Sorry, Mom, I just thought it would be better if we could talk without any adults around. You know. Molly might feel weird about you hanging around."

"No problem," she said. "I understand."

Mrs. Weaver waited around until Molly arrived and then went out to get an early dinner for the boys.

But convincing Mrs. Weaver to leave had been a lot easier than convincing Molly Vickers that it had been Kyle Patrick, her dance date, who left the horrible note and picture. It was Kevin, she pointed out, who had said he didn't want her on the team. Kyle hadn't said anything about it. It had been Kevin who had been seen walking around the lockers earlier that day.

All true. But as Atticus explained everything away, Molly began to frown. A lot. She was thinking.

"You really think?" she started and then shook her head. "No, it couldn't be him." She continued to shake her head, unable to believe what they were telling her. "No, you guys are way off on this."

"But what if you were able to get Kyle to admit to it?" Atticus asked, causing Molly to laugh.

"Well, if he did do it, why would he admit to it? He's got the whole school hating Kevin. I mean, if he did do it, which I don't think he did."

"Okay, then, if he's innocent, we've got nothing to lose, right?" Atticus reasoned.

"Yeah," she said slowly, "except the fact that Kyle will know that we thought he did it. No, I don't want to do that."

"What if I told you there might be a way to find out if it was Kyle without him ever knowing anyone thought it was him? That way, if we're wrong and you're right, Kyle will never even know we had this conversation. But," Atticus said, waving a finger in the air, "if Kevin is really innocent, wouldn't you want to know about it?"

Molly looked from one boy to the other, raising her eyebrows. A slow smile crept over her face as she thought about it.

"And Kyle would never know about it?"

"If you do it right, he'll never know about it," Atticus nodded.

"If *I* do it right? What do I have to do?" She sat back suddenly. Trevor and Atticus both smiled at each other. This was going to be fun. This was going to be a lot of fun.

★ ★ ★

The Conclusion

★ ★ ★

THE TOILET PAPER CAPER

THE beauty of cliques, and there were rarely any, was that something like the TPing of Kevin Thurston's house could be common knowledge among all the jocks and cheerleaders yet be completely unknown to anyone else. Using the power of Amy Loe, word that Kevin Thurston's house was going to be TPed for what he did to Molly Vickers and the Cougars traveled fast. Through the proper channels, almost everyone said they would join in. Everyone, it seemed, was still pretty mad about Kevin getting himself thrown off the team and, thereby, causing the worst Cougar football season in years.

As soon as word spread around the school, Molly invited Kyle Patrick to come along. He feigned disinterest, saying he didn't feel quite right about it, but with two more "oh, come ons," Kyle was in! Secretly, Atticus wondered if

Kyle was feeling a little guilty about the whole thing and didn't want to make it worse by TPing an innocent guy. But, true to his nature, he was more interested in being popular with the crowd, so he went along.

The date and time were set. Amy Loe spread the word that everyone would meet on the corner of Spring and Olde North Church (which was were Kevin lived) at precisely 11:30 p.m. "How you get there is your business, but bring plenty of toilet paper because the Cougars are going to get Kevin good!"

• • • •

At 11:43 p.m. there were no less than 20 kids hovering beneath the Spring and Olde North Church sign, not one of them talking. It was funny to see such a large group of notoriously loud teens all being so quiet, using sign language with one another. The whispering didn't actually begin until they spotted Trevor pushing Atticus down the street toward them.

What's he doing here?

He's going to get us caught!

You can't go TPing in a wheelchair! What? Is he crazy?

What are they doing here? Who told them about this?

As predicted, Kyle stepped forward, ready to tell Atticus and Trevor to go home, when Molly pulled him to the side and whispered to him. Causing a fight now, she warned him, would be too noisy. Besides, the more people to throw toilet paper, the better, and anyone who saw Atticus had to be impressed. On either handle of his chair were two bags stuffed full of toilet paper, as well as a large bag sitting in his lap. Whoever ran out of toilet paper could come to Atticus for a fresh supply.

"Car!" someone whisper-yelled, and everyone scuttled away, hiding in bushes and behind cars while the car lights cruised by. Kyle, Molly, Atticus, and Trevor all wound up hiding behind the same parked pickup. This caused great distress for Kyle, who scowled at both Atticus and Trevor.

"What are you doing here?" he hissed. "No one invited you."

"No one had to," Trevor shot back. "We hate Kevin Thurston all by ourselves."

Kyle Patrick thought about this for a minute as the car passed.

"For whatever reason you think you've got rights to TP his house," Atticus added, "we've got more. Kevin Thurston's been making my life miserable for years. He's got this one coming," he said, patting the rolls of toilet paper sitting on his lap.

David Lepac jumped up from behind a bush and waved everyone on. The coast was clear.

On cue, Molly ran ahead to the others, momentarily leaving Kyle alone with Trevor and Atticus. From where they were, they could see streams of white flying through the air. Molly was busily running around some of the bushes that adorned the Thurston driveway and front walk while Amy Loe and some of the other cheerleaders wrapped toilet paper around a car or two.

"Man, you pulled off the perfect crime," Trevor said to Kyle. Kyle had been pulling a roll of toilet paper from his jacket and was ready to run off and join his friends when Trevor's voice stopped him cold.

"What?"

"The crime," Trevor said. "The perfect crime." Trevor smiled over at Atticus to let Kyle know that Atticus knew about the crime as well.

"It's okay, though. It's cool with us." Trevor raised one hand up into the air and put his other hand over his heart.

"I don't know what you're talking about," Kyle snapped. He couldn't have looked more disgusted with Atticus or Trevor. It was clear that even talking to them brought him great pain.

"Hey, look, you don't have to play with us. We hate Kevin, and watching him get kicked off the football team was like the best thing we ever saw," Trevor said. Kyle shook his head and started to walk away, but Trevor stayed in stride with him. There was no way for Atticus to keep up with them as Olde North Church was on a slight incline. It was enough of a hill to slow Atticus down. But Atticus was not worried. He and Trevor had been over the routine enough times.

Trevor would tell Kyle that he had been in the main hall for an early meeting with Mr. Bradley about the chess club. It was geeky enough by Kyle's standards to be believable. In Kyle's mind, why else would a kid be early for school? Then Trevor would tell Kyle he had seen him putting the sign over Molly's locker.

If they were right, and Atticus was sure they were, Kyle just might believe Trevor's bluff.

If all went well, they would be able to convince Kyle Patrick that they, Atticus and Trevor (the number one victims of Kevin Thurston and his evil ways), thought it was funny that Kevin Thurston was now the number one bad guy at Walnut Middle School. It couldn't have happened to a nicer guy!

Atticus huffed and puffed his way up the hill, looking after Trevor and Kyle. The black sky was lit up with great streaks of white. It almost looked like fireworks as the rolls of toilet paper silently sailed through the air, decorating all the trees, shrubs, and bushes.

Atticus stopped to appreciate the moment. The beauty of all of this was, if Trevor got Kyle to confess, they would be able to clear Kevin's name. They would be the heroes who saved the Cougar football team. This, of course, was their original goal. If that failed or it proved to be that Kyle Patrick was innocent, however, they got to TP Kevin Thurston's house anyway. And a fine job everyone was doing.

Suddenly, Trevor turned toward Atticus, coughing.

The signal.

Atticus fumbled with the bag on his lap.

Beneath the bag of toilet paper, he held his old G.I. Joe walkie-talkie he had gotten for his eighth birthday. While the thing really didn't work anymore, just by flipping the on and off button a couple of times, enough static was created on the other walkie-talkie.

He flipped it a couple of times for good measure and waited.

"Car!" someone whisper-yelled. Two seconds later, the outside porch light to the Thurston house flipped on, and everyone scattered like bugs, diving out of sight. Cheerleaders and football players ran wildly down the street, dispersing on Spring Street. Only Atticus and Trevor hung back in the shadows behind a parked car. They could see Molly off in the distance, dragging Kyle along with her, making sure he made it out of the neighborhood.

Slowly, a minivan turned up Olde North Church and came to a stop. Kevin Thurston stepped out onto his porch and looked around. Mrs. Weaver rolled down her window from the car and waved at Kevin, who waved back. She had made the call to Kevin so that he could flip on the light and clear everyone out.

"Okay, coast is clear," Trevor said, pushing Atticus to the minivan. Mission accomplished.

Once they loaded Atticus's chair into the van, Mrs. Weaver hopped back in behind the wheel and turned down Spring.

"Well," she said excitedly, looking into the rearview mirror. "I almost blew it the first time, didn't I? I drove by the first time too early." She was chuckling to herself. "I saw about five people dive out of sight. Boy, if I had really been a car just driving along, I would have called the police. Your friends are terrible hiders."

"They're not our friends," Trevor said, the voice of reason.

"I hope I called at the right time," Mrs. Weaver went on, turning around to see Atticus in the back seat. "That was the signal, wasn't it?"

He nodded. It was hard not to smile at her. Clearly, she was having such a good time. She was in the sting operation and was loving it. How many other moms would have agreed to this? Not only did she allow Atticus to go out TPing, she even supplied the ride and the toilet paper.

"Well," Trevor said, wrestling with his jacket and pulling out the tape recorder. "I got it!"

"You did?" Atticus turned on him, suddenly forgetting all about his mother. He had hoped this would happen, but in all honestly, he wasn't expecting anything to come of this adventure except seeing Kevin's house get TPed. "What did he say? What did he say?" Atticus could barely contain himself.

"Listen." Trevor smiled proudly to himself. He rewound the tape and pressed the play button. While the conversation between Trevor and Kyle unfolded, Mrs. Weaver drove through the neighborhood. In the darkness of the van, with no sounds except those emanating from the tiny tape recorder, Atticus, his mother, and Trevor held their breath.

The tape replayed a conversation Atticus already knew.

"No one invited you." That was Kyle.

"No one had to. We hate Kevin Thurston all by ourselves." That was Trevor. Mrs. Weaver chuckled.

"Good one," she said. Atticus shushed her, and Trevor fast-forwarded the tape a little. Atticus chewed on his fingernails nervously.

"So what if I did? You can't prove anything," came Kyle's voice, and Atticus took in a deep breath. It was better than he had ever hoped.

"Who's trying to prove anything?" came Trevor's voice. Atticus leaned forward. It was difficult to hear because of the rustling of Trevor's jacket. "I'm telling you it was a good deal. I just can't believe you thought of it."

Nothing.

"What's happening now?" Atticus whispered, and Trevor shook his head, trying to remember.

"I think he was thinking. Yeah, he was looking at me, trying to decide if I was for real."

"I didn't," came Kyle's voice. "It wasn't my idea at all. I just kind of, you know, helped out."

"For real? Who else? Man, we ought to form a 'We Hate Kevin' club. I used to think he was so popular, but not anymore," Trevor said back.

"That was a good one." Atticus gave Trevor a nudge.

"Shhh." Trevor waved his hand, pointing down to the tiny tape recorder he held. Kyle's voice came back, now clearer than ever.

"I got a buddy who set it up," Kyle confided.

As they drove around town, Atticus, his mom, and Trevor listened as though they were hearing the greatest secret of all time!

• • • •

When they finally got home, the phone rang. It was Molly Vickers.

"Did you get it?" she whispered into the phone.

"Yeah, we got it," Atticus told her. The phone was quiet for a moment.

"He admitted it?" she asked. Her voice seemed strained. It had to hurt to know that Kyle Patrick could do something so mean and then pretend to be her friend.

"Yeah."

"I want to hear it," she insisted. "I want to hear him say it."

"Tomorrow," Atticus offered.

"Okay, I have to go. They think I'm calling my parents,"

"Where's Kyle?" Atticus wanted to know.

"We all ran back here to Amy's. Then the guys took off from here," she said. "I guess he's home now." She sounded disgusted.

"Okay," Atticus said, relaxing a little. "Then, tomorrow."

"Tomorrow," Molly whispered and hung up. She, like all the other girls, had been spending the night at Amy Loe's. It was the only way to get all the girls together to TP Kevin's house.

"What did she say?" Mrs. Weaver asked.

"Well," Atticus said, setting down the phone. "She wasn't happy." He was sorry about that, but she needed to know the truth.

"Well, she needed to know the truth," Mrs. Weaver piped in, and Atticus smiled at her. They thought alike. "But for now," she said, doing a little happy jig in the middle of the kitchen, "let's celebrate. Who wants ice cream and cake and everything else that's bad for us?"

Atticus nodded. On Monday they would take their tape recording to Mr. Gulf. The tape would clear Kevin's name, get him back on the team, and make sure the Cougars would start winning again. Kyle Patrick and his good buddy Martin Williams from the Blendon team would be in more trouble than they had bargained for. And Molly would know who her real friends were, including one Atticus Weaver and one Trevor Smith. Not only did she know their names, she would be thankful to them. And, best of all, Atticus had been right. He had believed Kevin was innocent when no one else believed him.

Life just couldn't get any better.

The phone rang again.

"You didn't have to TP the whole house," came Kevin's voice over the phone. Atticus looked over to Trevor and grinned. Life couldn't get any better, and yet it just did!

THE OUTCASTS

IN *To Kill a Mockingbird*, Atticus lost his case in trying to protect Tom. But Atticus promised him that he would file an appeal. He promised Tom that they weren't finished. He said that they would go to a higher court. He did that because he knew Tom was innocent. He could have stopped right then and there, but he didn't. Atticus Finch believed in the importance of helping out a fellow human being. But something terrible happened to Tom, and he died.

It was a terrible ending for a nice man who was falsely accused of a crime he didn't commit. Kevin Thurston's story was much different, much better. Once he was put back on the team, he was able to lead his team to victory. He was popular again, and he went to the dance with Molly Vickers.

Kyle Patrick was suspended from school and kicked off the team. Once word got around about how he had tried to set up his one-time best friend, his career at Walnut was finished. There were rumors that he was withdrawing from school and his parents were going to send him to a private school.

It seemed to be the perfect ending, which was a funny thing to Atticus. He sat watching everyone, thinking about how everything had played itself out.

The beginning. What was the beginning? He had wanted so desperately to be considered like everyone else, even when that meant getting punched in the face. It seemed ridiculous now, but he had wanted a black eye more than anything else in the world. He had wanted the courtesy of being identified as the first strain of tomato. He had wanted to be popular. He had wanted to be the hero of Walnut Middle School so everyone would like him. He had wanted to be the guy who could save Kevin Thurston and be at the dance with Molly Vickers.

And here he was. At the dance, watching everyone.

Things had changed so much for him and

Trevor. And yet, nothing had changed at all.

The geeks were flocking around the refreshment area, looking like they were engaged in whatever interesting conversations they were engaged in when, in truth, they wanted desperately to be asked to dance, or be able to ask someone to dance, or just plain be able to dance. They all wondered why they were there. Why had they even come? It happened that one geek had said he would go, so the other geeks agreed to go as well. There was safety in gaggles of geeks.

The freaks were few in number. Freaks could be seen at rallies because they had to be there, but few freaks bothered to come to the dances. Those who did hung back, heckling the brave ones who made it to the dance floor.

That, of course, would mostly be the beauties and the cheerleaders, with a few jocks here and there. Mostly, though, the jocks hung back on the farthest, darkest wall and talked loudly to one another. If it appeared that they were having a really good time, there would be no need for them to actually stop what they were doing, dance, and risk being made fun of by the sparsely scattered freaks. The geeks wouldn't dare.

The outcasts didn't care. They were there for whatever reasons they were there. Curiosity. Boredom. Or, in the case of Atticus Weaver and his good buddy Trevor Smith, by invitation.

They had been invited by Molly Vickers, Kevin Thurston, and all of their popular friends. It was everything Atticus had ever wanted. He was part of the "in crowd." As Trevor had mused earlier, his high school career was set.

It was a funny thing, all of this.

When the townspeople had tried to come into town and lynch poor old Tom even before his trial, Atticus Finch stopped them. He stood up against everything that was wrong, and he was very unpopular, but he didn't care. He was doing what he knew was right, and that was that.

It was then that Atticus realized that Atticus Finch was an outcast, as well. He wasn't one of the popular ones, and he didn't care. He was brave, and he was a hero, and he was an outcast. He did what he did because it was right, and it didn't bother him if people talked about him. At least, he didn't care about the townspeople. He did care about Tom's people because they were kind and good and real.

"Hey, Atticus!" A booming voice broke through his thoughts, and Atticus saw Connor Pearson waving him over to their crowd.

It was everything he had ever wanted.

And yet, it was a funny thing to see Kevin Thurston right smack in the middle of all of his buddies, acting as if nothing was different. Had he forgotten how they all had turned on him in his time of need? Had he forgotten how none of them had wanted anything to do with him? But now they were all flocking around him.

Even as they all called Atticus over to them, he couldn't seem to make himself go. Something was holding him back. He had thought for so long that all he ever wanted to be was in the popular crowd, but now it didn't feel right. It didn't fit. Something was holding him back.

Just then, Kathy Quigley strolled past the group of jocks, and there followed a loud "moo" call. Kathy Quigley was a pretty big girl and was teased a lot about it. But she was also very, very smart. Atticus knew because they were in many of the same classes together. She had won plenty of awards herself in the annual science fairs. In fact, she was usually Atticus's stiffest competition.

He watched Kathy as she pretended not to hear what was being said about her. Some girls tried to tell the boys to stop, but it was in that whiny way that told Atticus they didn't really mean it. *Pigly Quigley!*

"Yo, Weaver!" Kevin Thurston called over to him again. Kevin was grinning hugely at Atticus, sincerely wanting him to join him and his friends. Atticus nodded back and looked around for Trevor.

Trevor was out on the floor dancing! For a moment, Atticus laughed out loud in disbelief. Kathy Quigley had cornered him and dragged him out there. He didn't want to be there but couldn't say no.

He was the worst dancer Atticus had ever seen in his life.

It was then that Atticus realized why his mother had named him after Atticus Finch. Not because he was going to be some great mystery solver or lawyer but because he was an outcast too.

He was brave, and he was a hero, and he would forever be an outcast, and he wouldn't have it any other way.